THE FOOD OF
BALI

Authentic Recipes from the Island of the Gods

Recipes by Heinz von Holzen & Lother Arsana

Food photography by Heinz von Holzen

Introduction and editing by Wendy Hutton

Produced in cooperation with the Grand Hyatt Bali

PERIPLUS
EDITIONS

Published by Periplus Editions (HK) Ltd.

Copyright © 1994 Periplus Editions (HK) Ltd.
ALL RIGHTS RESERVED
Printed in the Republic of Singapore
ISBN: 0-945971-96-6
Address all inquiries and comments to:
   Periplus (Singapore) Pte. Ltd.
   Farrer Road P.O. Box 115, Singapore 9128

Publisher: Eric Oey
Design: Peter Ivey
Marketing Director: Julian Sale
Production: Mary Chia

Photo Credits
Photos by Heinz von Holzen except
pages 4–5, 13, 19, 22, 25 by Rio Helmi
pages 8, 10, 12, 14–15 by R. Ian Lloyd
page 16, 21 by Eric Oey
page 23 by Fiona Nichols

Distributors
Indonesia:
   C.V. Java Books, Box 55, JKCP, Jakarta 10510.
Japan:
   Charles E Tuttle Inc., 21-13, Seki 1-Chome,
   Tama-ku, Kawasaki, Kanagawa 214.
Singapore and Malaysia:
   Berkeley Books Pte. Ltd.
   Farrer Road P.O. Box 115, Singapore 9128.
Thailand:
   Asia Books Co. Ltd
   5 Sukhumvit Soi 61, Sukhumvit Road, P.O. Box 40
   Bangkok 10110.
United Kingdom:
   GeoCenter U.K. Ltd.,
   The Viables Center, Harrow Way,
   Basingstoke, Hampshire RG22 4BJ.

Dedication
This book is dedicated to the people of Bali, who helped show me the meaning of life, and to my wife, Puji, and son, Fabian.

Acknowledgements
I would like to thank all those people whose whole-hearted support made this book possible. First and foremost, Mr Peter Stettler, General Manager of Grand Hyatt Bali, for his unfailing and enthusiastic assistance throughout the preparation of this book. Cherrie and Desmond Hill offered continuous personal support and photographic advice. Sharon Antis patiently spent hours helping put the recipes into shape. My thanks to all the chefs of the Grand Hyatt Bali, in particular, Wayan Widiana and Martin Graham and his team, who were responsible for the preparation of the food. A special thank you to Brent Hesslyn, both for introductions and for the creation of all tableware used in the book. Thanks also to Puri Sakana Antiques Art Gallery and owner I Wayan Dupa Suciptra and woodcarver Ida Bagus Tilem for providing all the carvings used in the photographs. Finally, I would like to thank my editor, Wendy Hutton, whose professional expertise and long experience with Southeast Asian cuisines helped bring the work of all of us to the final stages.

—Heinz von Holzen

All ceramics appearing in this book were designed and produced by Jenggala Keramik, Batujimbar, Sanur, P.O. Box 3025, Denpasar, Bali, Indonesia. Telephone: 62 361 288147; facsimile: 62 361 287930.

Contents

Part One: Food in Bali

Sustenance and sacrifice:
the island cuisine in context

The extravagant beauty of Bali and its vibrant culture first captured the imagination of the world in the 1930s, when it was visited by a few adventurous Dutch colonists, artists and the international jet set (who in those days actually travelled by ship). Since the arrival of mass tourism during the 1970s, hundreds of thousands of tourists have descended upon the "Island of the Gods", yet most leave without having eaten one single meal of genuine Balinese food. How could this peculiar situation come about?

Bali, then made up of nine separate kingdoms, was conquered by the Dutch in 1908. This was later than most of the other islands of the Dutch East Indies which, together with Bali, now make up modern-day Indonesia. As early as the 8th century, Hinduism and Buddhism arrived on the island. Although Java converted to Islam in the 16th century, Bali has remained to this day staunchly devoted to the Balinese form of the Hindu religion, which continues to govern every aspect of life on the island.

With its volcanoes periodically scattering the land with fertile ash, rivers watering the rice fields and its balmy tropical climate, the Balinese are able to grow a superb array of fresh produce. Food, like everything else in Bali, is a matter of contrast. Just as there is male and female, good and evil, night and day, there is ordinary daily food and festival food intended for the gods. Regular daily food is based on rice, with a range of spicy side dishes including vegetables, a small amount of meat or fish, and a variety of condiments.

Rice and the accompanying dishes are cooked in the morning, after a trip to the market, and left in the kitchen for the family to help themselves whenever they're hungry. Daily meals, which are eaten only twice a day (with plenty of snacks in between) are not sociable affairs. The Balinese normally eat quickly, silently and alone, often in a corner of the kitchen or perhaps sitting on the edge of one of the open pavilions in the family courtyard. In contrast with this matter-of-fact approach to daily food, food prepared for festive occasions is elaborate, often exquisitely decorated and eaten communally.

Dining out is not a social custom, therefore unless the visitor is invited into a Balinese home, or samples festive favourites such as spit-roasted pig or stuffed duck roasted in banana leaf offered at a tourist restaurant, he or she is not likely to experience real Balinese food. Nevertheless, the spices, seasonings and secret touches that make Balinese food unique are just awaiting discovery.

Pages 4–5: Mount Agung, Bali's most sacred mountain, dominates the landscape of eastern Bali.
***Opposite**: Balinese meal of Sate Lilit (top), Yellow Rice, Urap and Grilled Chicken (right) and Black Rice Pudding with fresh rambutans (left).*

Garden of the Gods

Tropical bounty in the shadow of volcanoes:
geography, climate and cultivation

Bali's landscape is characterised by abundance: thousands of verdant rice fields, graceful coconut palms and a myriad of tropical fruit trees, coffee plantations and even vineyards make up the cultivated areas. On the slopes of the mountains lush tangles of vines and creepers link huge trees, many dripping with orchids and ferns. It is not hard to understand why the island is often described as "the morning of the world," "island of the gods" and "the enchanted paradise."

Rice terraces cannot function without irrigation. The irrigation cooperatives, or subaks, ensure that sufficient water is available year-round.

Lying between 8 and 9 degrees south of the equator, Bali is only 144 kilometres east to west and 80 kilometres north to south. Its extraordinary richness is the result of a combination of factors. The island, and most of Indonesia, lies above the join of two of the earth's seven tectonic plates and the towering volcanoes that dominate the landscape are responsible for much of Bali's fertility. Occasional eruptions, while potentially destructive, paradoxically increase fertility as they scatter rich ash and debris over the soil.

The tall mountains (Gunung Agung is 3,142 metres, and neighbouring Gunung Batur 1,717 metres) help generate heavy downpours of rain, which collects in a number of springs and lakes. The water flowing down the mountain slopes creates rivers which carve deep ravines as they make their way down to the sea.

Bali experiences two seasons, a hot wet season from November to March, and a cooler dry season from April to October. Long periods of sunshine and adequate rainfall create a monsoon forest (as opposed to rainforest, which grows in tropical regions without a dry season). Natural vegetation, however, covers only about a quarter of Bali (mainly in the west). The rest of the countryside has been extensively modified through cultivation.

The Balinese eat only very small amounts of meat, poultry or fish. Rice is the centrepiece of every meal, accompanied by a variety of vegetables, spicy condiments or sambals, crunchy extras such as peanuts, crisp-fried shallots, fried *tempeh* (a fermented soya-bean cake) or one of dozens of types of crisp wafer (*krupuk*). Although rice is the staple, certain other starchy foods such as cassava, sweet potatoes and maize are also eaten, sometimes mixed with rice, not just as an economy measure (they cost less) but because they provide a variation of flavour.

Many of the leafy greens enjoyed by the Balinese are gathered wild, such as the young shoots of trees found in the family compound (starfruit is one favourite), or young fern tips and other edible greens found along the lanes or edges of the padi fields. Immature fruits like the jackfruit and papaya are also used as vegetables. The Balinese cook uses mature coconut almost daily, grating it to add to vegetables, frying it with seasonings to make a condiment, or squeezing the grated flesh with water to make coconut milk for sauces which accompany both sweet and savoury dishes.

Although the seas surrounding the island are rich in fish, the Balinese, even those living near the coast, eat surprisingly little seafood. Mountains are regarded as the abode of the gods and therefore holy, while the lowest place of all—the sea—is said to be the haunt of evil spirits and a place of mysterious power. On a more pragmatic level, the coastline of Bali is dangerous for boats and possesses few natural harbours.

The majority of the fish caught are a type of sardine, tuna and mackerel. Fresh fish is available in coastal markets and the capital, Denpasar, but owing to the limited availability of refrigeration, other markets sell these fish either preserved in brine or dried and salted, like *ikan teri*, a popular anchovy. Sea turtles have long been regarded as a special food and are eaten on festive occasions along the coast and in the south of Bali.

A beautiful tan coloured cow with a white rear end that makes it look as if it has sat in talcum powder is being successfully raised in Bali, although beef itself is seldom eaten by the Balinese.

Pork is the favourite meat and appears on most festive occasions. Duck is also featured frequently on Balinese festival menus, usually stuffed with spices and steamed before being roasted on charcoal or minced to make satay.

The Balinese eat creatures that not everyone would consider candidates for the table, including dragonflies, small eels, frogs, crickets, flying foxes and certain types of larvae. Visitors are advised to dismiss any preconceptions and sample whatever is offered.

Rice, the Gift of Dewi Sri

Soul food, the life force and the rice revolution

Terraced rice fields climb the slopes of Bali's most holy mountain, Gunung Agung, like steps to heaven. When tender seedlings are first transplanted, they are slender spikes of green mirrored in the silver waters of the irrigated fields. Within a couple of months the fields become solid sheets of emerald which turn slowly to rich gold as the grains ripen. Although irrigated rice fields cover no more than 20% of Bali's arable land, the overwhelming impression is a landscape of endless fertile padi fields slashed by deep ravines and backed by dramatic mountains.

Rice, the staple food of the Balinese, nourishes both body and soul. As elsewhere in Asia, the word for cooked rice (*nasi*) is synonymous with the word for meal. If a Balinese has a bowl of noodles it's regarded as just a snack—without rice, it cannot be considered a meal.

Red, black, white and yellow are the four sacred colours in Bali, each representing a particular manifestation of God. Although the majority of rice cultivated on the island is white, reddish-brown rice and black glutinous rice are also grown. The vivid juice of the turmeric root is added when yellow rice is needed on festive occasions.

A big plate of steamed white rice (usually eaten at room temperature) is the usual way rice is presented, although it appears in countless other guises. The most common Balinese breakfast is a snack of boiled rice-flour dumplings sweetened with palm sugar syrup and freshly grated coconut. All types of rice are made into various other sweet desserts and cakes.

Dewi Sri, the Rice Goddess who personifies the life force, is undoubtedly the most worshipped deity in Bali. The symbol representing Dewi Sri is seen time and again: an hourglass figure often made from rice stalks, woven from coconut leaves, engraved or painted onto wood, made out of old Chinese coins, or hammered out of metal. Shrines made of bamboo or stone honouring Dewi Sri are erected in every rice field.

Rice cultivation determines the rhythm of village life and daily work, as well as the division of labour

between men and women. Every stage of the rice cycle is accompanied by age-old rituals. The dry season, from April to September, makes irrigation essential for the two annual crops. An elaborate system channelling water from lakes, rivers and springs across countless padis is controlled by irrigation cooperatives known as *subak*. Consisting of all the landowners of a particular district, the *subak* is responsible not only for the construction and maintenance of canals, aqueducts and dams and the distribution of water, but also coordinates the planting and organises ritual offerings and festivals. The *subak* system is extremely efficient and computer studies have found that, for Bali, its methods cannot be further improved.

The so-called rice revolution has had an enormous impact on Bali, as it has on all Asian rice-growing countries. For over twenty years, the International Rice Research Institute, headquartered in the Philippines, has been developing high-yield rice strains resistant to disease and pests. Bali's traditional rice variety, *beras Bali*, is a graceful plant which reaches a height of around 1.4 metres (56 inches). It has a superior flavour and many Balinese willingly pay up to four times the price of ordinary rice for it. But the most widely used new rice in Bali is the unima-

An offering to Dewi Sri, the rice goddess, includes a symbolic depiction of the goddess herself. A representation of the life force, she is the most widely-worshipped deity in Bali.

ginatively named IR36, developed by the IRRI.

This so-called "miracle" rice takes roughly 120 days to mature compared to the 150 days required for *beras Bali*. It is now grown in 90% of Bali's rice fields. Traditionally, the long stems of *beras Bali* were tied together in sheaves, carried to the granary for storing, then pounded in a big wooden mortar to dislodge the husks when rice was needed. The stems of IR36, however, are short (half the height of *beras Bali*) and the grains easily dislodged. Thus, threshing has to take place immediately after harvesting. Certain traditional rice harvesting practices, including the construction of granaries, are dying out with the introduction of the new varieties. The Balinese acknowledge the superior yield and growth rate of the new plants: in 1979, Bali almost doubled the amount of rice it had harvested a decade earlier.

Since 1984, Indonesia has been able to provide sufficient rice to feed its burgeoning population, and can now concentrate on developing varieties better suited to local conditions. The Department of Agriculture is now experimenting with rice strains that can, it is hoped, eventually be reconciled with the basic foundations of Balinese culture. Dewi Sri, it seems certain, will continue to be honoured and her blessings sought for many more generations.

Daily Life in Bali

Harmony and cooperation within the village compound

The rhythm of the day in a typical Balinese family compound is ruled by the rice harvest, governed by tradition and watched over by the gods. Several generations usually live together in the compound, which is laid out in accordance with esoteric Balinese principles and surrounded by a mud or brick wall. The holiest part of the land (that which faces the mountains) is reserved for the various shrines honouring the gods and ancestral spirits.

Beyond this enclosed area are a series of other pavilions or rooms used as sleeping and living quarters, with the kitchen or *paon* and the bathroom near the least auspicious part of the property–that closest to the sea. Farthest of all from the holy area one finds the family pigsty (there is always at least one occupant being fattened up for the next important feast) and the rubbish pit.

Flowering trees and shrubs (a source of blooms for the daily offerings) are dotted about the compound, while the gardens at the back often contain several fruit trees: papayas, bananas (their leaves essential for wrapping food) and coconut palms, among others.

The women are always occupied, cooking, cleaning, washing clothes, sweeping and preparing offerings. Older women often take the daily offerings around the compound, setting them before the various shrines before anyone has their first meal of the day, as well as performing other tasks such as feeding the pigs, weaving offerings, making special rice cakes and keeping an eye on the youngest children.

The old men who are no longer fit for work in the fields pass the day slicing strips of bamboo and shaping them into baskets, repairing tools or utensils, and doing odd jobs about the yard. When nothing remains to be done, or they feel like taking a break, they wander off to a nearby *warung* (simple local store) for a cup of coffee and a chat with friends.

Towards the end of day, when it's cooler and the younger men have returned from the fields, they may all gather to watch a cockfight. Although gambling is forbidden throughout Indonesia, there's

Left:
Making the daily offerings in the family compound.
Pages 14–15:
The market at Denpasar, Bali's capital, is the largest and most colourful on the island.

A Chili pepper vendor in the vegetable market at Batur sorts her wares.

This pavilion is also where utensils and other objects involved in worship are stored (generally in the rafters) and where ceremonies involving rites of passage, such as weddings and tooth filings, take place. (The Balinese abhor pointed canine teeth which they say makes them look like animals, and they are filed down by priests usually when youths reach puberty.)

Culinary skills are passed on from mother to daughter down the generations. Girls frequently undertake the daily task of peeling of shallots and garlic, slicing and chopping seasonings, and grinding spice pastes with a mortar and pestle. They are also entrusted with cutting banana leaves and trimming them into shape so that they can be filled with food, folded and secured with a sliver of bamboo.

The complex ingredients for Balinese food and ritual offerings are all committed to memory, no Balinese woman ever needs to consult a cookbook for a Balinese recipe, although a modern woman might follow a recipe for dishes from other Indonesian regions.

Many families now have television sets, and most *bale banjar*, or community centres, also have a set where anyone can gather to watch programmes in Indonesian, English or Balinese. Early evenings are also the time when the various cooperative organisations meet for discussions and planning, and there are also informal "drinking clubs", where the men meet over a glass of *tuak* (palm brew).

By about 9 pm, doors of the enclosure are closed against any malign spirits that may be wandering in the night and the only lights to be seen in the village are those of twinkling fireflies.

always a corner of every village where this traditional sport goes on, with scant regard for the law.

Young girls learn the tasks of a woman in the same way they learn to dance—by imitating their elders from a very early age, and perfecting technique over time. The *bale gede* is usually where women gather to prepare temple offerings, including weaving young coconut palm leaves into trays, baskets, or complex hangings.

At Home with Ibu Rani

A day in the life of
a Balinese cook

Mangku Gerjar, an elderly priest from the village of Ubud in central Bali, lives with his extended family in a typical compound. The compound houses a total of thirteen people: he and his wife, Ibu Kawi, their three married sons, and their wives and children. Mangku Gerjar's youngest son, Nyoman Bahula, and his wife, Rani, are modern Balinese, having only two children, Rudi and Lies.

In the morning, once the children have gone to school, Ibu Rani sets off to market. (*Ibu*, a polite Indonesian term of address for a married woman, is not actually used among the Balinese, who have a very complex system of names.) By 7 am the market is already crowded. Rani bypasses mounds of brilliant flowers and coconut-leaf offering trays to select a kilo of purple-skinned sweet potatoes. From piles of vivid leafy green vegetables, she picks out a couple of bundles of water convolvulus or *kangkung.* Next into the shopping basket goes a paper twist of raw peanuts and a leaf-wrapped slab of fermented soya bean cake (*tempeh*).

Rani pauses by some enamel basins full of fish in brine, changes her mind and settles for a bag of tiny, frantically wriggling eels caught in the rice fields, then goes to the meat stall and buys a piece of pork and a small plastic bag of fresh pig's blood.

The basics of today's meals already purchased, Ibu Rani heads for the spice stalls. Mounds of purplish shallots, pearl-white garlic and chillies ranging from long red *tabia lombok* to the popular short, chunky red and yellow *tabia Bali,* fiery little red and green bird's-eye chillies compete with piles of innocuous-looking roots hiding their rich fragrances. There's familiar ginger; its relative, *laos* or greater galangal; lesser galangal or *kencur* (known to the Balinese as *cekuh*), with its white, crunchy and flavoursome flesh, and finally vivid yellow turmeric, the most pungent of all.

Fragrant screwpine or *pandan* leaf, the faintly flavoured *salam* leaf, the small but headily scented kaffir lime and its double leaf, spears of lemon grass and sprigs of lemon-scented basil, all promise magic in the kitchen. Like the emphatic tones of a

Ibu Rani (right) with Mbok Made (left) and Kadek Astri Anggreni (centre) weaving a jejaitan *from palm leaves in their Ubud family compound. The* jejaitan *is the base mat upon which temple offerings are placed.*

large gong, the odour of dried shrimp paste from a nearby stall assails the senses.

Ibu Rani pauses for her daily glass of *jamu*, a herbal brew which she says keeps her body "clean inside", then buys breakfast for herself and her husband: a few small moist rice cakes or *jaja*, sprinkled with fresh coconut and splashed with palm sugar syrup. Hoisting her basket onto her head, Rani then walks home.

Within the compound, sounds of grinding can already be heard from the other two kitchens. Pulling out the morning's purchases, Rani gets to work, peeling and chopping seasonings for the leaf-wrapped food *tum*. "I make *tum* almost every day," she explains, "sometimes it's with eels, with a little meat or perhaps some chicken. Today, I'm going to use pork."

An earthy smell permeates the kitchen as she finely chops shallots, ginger, garlic, chillies, fresh turmeric, *kencur* roots and *salam* leaves. Next, she removes scraps of gristle from the piece of pork and throws them out for the chickens. The pork is then deftly minced into paste with a cleaver, and mixed with chopped seasoning, a big pinch of salt, a splash of oil and the pig's blood.

Large spoonfuls of this mixture are spread onto a square of banana leaf, carefully folded, then secured with a slender bamboo skewer. By this time, the rice—which had slivers of sweet potato added halfway through cooking—is turned out into a colander. The leaf-wrapped bundles of pork are set in the same steamer used for the rice and put over boiling water to cook.

Pulling out her saucer-shaped stone mortar, Rani gets ready to grind the spices for seasoning the *tempeh*. "Don't bother to peel the garlic," she cautions, "there's no need, the skins will fall off when it's cooking." Like most Balinese cooks, she sees no need for fussy refinements.

The ground turmeric root, garlic, salt and white peppercorns are mixed with a little water and massaged into the protein-rich tempeh, which is left to stand for about half an hour before frying. Rani fries the peanuts in her wok, reserving some as a crunchy garnish and then grinds the remainder with toasted shrimp paste and chillies to make a tangy sauce to be mixed with the blanched green vegetable (*kangkung*). The eels are drained, salted and cleaned before also being fried in hot oil. Their crunchiness and flavour is later improved by tossing them in the wok with chilli paste.

Finally, everything is cooked and ready. The colander of rice is covered and left on the bench, and the remaining dishes set in a cupboard for family members to help themselves to throughout the day.

Lavish Gifts for the Gods

Festival foods serve as offerings,
works of art and meals for mortals

Food in Bali is literally deemed fit for the gods. Every day of the year, the spirits whose shrines occupy the forecourt of every Balinese family compound are presented with offerings of flowers, food, holy water and incense. The offerings serve to honour the spirits and ensure that they safeguard the health and prosperity of the family. Even malicious spirits are pacified with small leaf trays of rice and salt which are put on the ground. These simple offerings are, without fail, presented before the whole family eats their first meal of the day.

At more elaborate temple festivals, brilliantly dressed women form processions as they bear towering offerings of fruits, flowers and food upon their heads. These elaborate temple offerings are virtually works of art, but have a deep symbolic significance which goes far beyond mere decoration.

A seemingly endless round of religious and private family celebrations ensures that the women—whose task it is to prepare such offerings—always spend some part of the day folding intricate baskets

Food art for the gods. A festival offering made from rice dough.

or trays, or preparing some of the more than sixty types of *jaja or* rice cakes essential for festivals. Young girls sit beside their elders who pass on the intricate art of cutting and folding young coconut-palm leaves, moulding fresh rice-dough into figures, colouring rice cakes and assembling the appropriate offerings for each occasion. Women working outside the home may purchase their offerings from a specialist *tukang banten* in a market, but they never fail to observe their ritual obligations.

Temple festivals and private celebrations, such as weddings or tooth filing ceremonies, don't just provide food for the gods—the mortals also get their share. Offerings brought to a temple are first purified by the priest, who sprinkles them with holy water while chanting prayers. Once the "essence" has been consumed by the gods, the edible portions are enjoyed by the families who brought them. Any stale left-overs, less-tasty morsels and stray grains of rice are eagerly consumed by the dogs, chickens, wild birds or even ants. Nothing goes to waste.

Apart from temple offerings prepared for the gods, special ritual foods are cooked solely for human consumption on important occasions. These foods are generally complex and require an enormous amount of co-operative effort to prepare. The Balinese, who normally eat very little protein food with their daily rice, consume comparatively large amounts of meat (generally pork or, in the south of the island, turtle) during festivals. Such feasts are a time for eating communally, generally seated on a mat on the ground of the temple, or within the family compound.

For a small family celebration, the food is prepared by the family involved. Larger feasts involve the whole *banjar*, or local community, the work being supervised by a ritual cooking specialist, who is invariably a man. There is a strict division of labour, with men being responsible

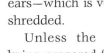

for butchering the pig or turtle, grating mountains of coconuts and grinding huge amounts of spices: all tasks which require considerable physical effort. The women perform the fiddly task of peeling and chopping the fresh seasonings, cooking the rice and preparing the vegetables.

The most famous festive dish is *lawar*. This is basically the firm-textured parts of a pig or turtle cut into slivers, mixed with pounded raw meat and fresh blood, and combined with a range of vegetables, seasonings and sauces. To Western tastes, the number of fiery hot chillies that goes into the *lawar* makes it positively incendiary!

A day before the *lawar* is prepared, the mammoth task of peeling hundreds of shallots and cloves of garlic, and scraping turmeric, *laos* and *kencur* roots has already begun, so that before dawn on the day of the festival, the preparation of the *lawar* can begin. A whole pig (generally raised at the back of the family compound) or a turtle is slaughtered, and some of the choicest meat is kept aside for chopping into a fine paste. The blood is also kept, mixed with lime juice to prevent it from coagulating. Another essential ingredient is a tough portion—if it is a turtle, it will be slivers of boiled cartilage, while in the case of a pig, the boiled ears—which is very finely shredded.

Unless the *lawar* is being prepared for a huge number of people, there will be plenty of leftover meat, which is prepared in a number of different ways: cooked with sweet soya sauce; simmered in a spicy coconut milk gravy and pounded and mixed with grated coconut and spice paste to make satays. Scrappy bits of pork are chopped finely, seasoned and packed into the reserved intestines and fried to make spicy sausages.

Various vegetables such as green beans, leaves from the starfruit tree or young fern tips, young jackfruit and green papaya are steamed and

Opposite:
Everyone works together to prepare festival food.
Left:
Rice being distributed after having been blessed by priests at the temple during the annual Perang Dewa or "War of the Gods" trance festival in Paksabali village in the regency of Klungkung.

A banana-leaf production line— offerings of meat are prepared in bulk.

has been roasted in the coals of the kitchen stove.

The task of mixing all these ingredients together to create the *lawar* is considered so specialised that either a ritual food specialist or the most senior male in the family compound is called in for the task. First into a huge enamelled bowl goes a handful of the shaved coconut, then a splash of blood is worked in by hand, turning the coconut bright red, the colour of Brahma (who is, along with Vishnu and Shiva, one of the three manifestations of the Hindu supreme being). One by one, other seasonings and ingredients are added and kneaded, creating four different types of *lawar*, each based on one of the four steamed vegetables.

The *lawar* is generally served on pieces of banana leaf (the original disposable plate!), and if there is any left over after a small family celebration, it is wrapped in banana leaf and steamed so that, in the absence of refrigeration, it will keep fresh until the evening or following day.

Another festive favourite that is also available on market days is the famous spit-roasted pig, *be guling celeng,* better known by its Indonesian name, *babi guling*. This can be made with a very young suckling pig, but normally in Bali a moderately sized pig is stuffed with a mixture of chillies, fragrant roots, herbs and spices, its skin liberally anointed with crushed turmeric dissloved in water. The pig is slowly roasted over a fire until the skin turns crisp and golden, and the flesh becomes meltingly tender and delicately flavoured by the stuffing. *Babi guling* is so delicious that it's not surprising that Balinese do not reserve it solely for festivals.

finely diced or grated. These are set out in readiness for the mixing of the *lawar*, together with a seasoned coconut milk sauce, bowls of finely chopped roots and chillies, roughly ground spices, slivers of palm sugar, wedges of fragrant kaffir lime, several types of chilli-based *sambal*, a bowl of salt, piles of crisp fried shallots, a bowl of fresh blood and the shredded cartilage. This is joined by the coarsely shaved flesh of a coconut which

Feasting the Ancestral Spirits

The Galungan festival—celebrating the triumph of good over evil

Galungan, one of the most important festivals in the Balinese calendar, is a time when the spirits of ancestors return to earth to live with the family. The spirits are said to descend five days before the festival begins, and return to heaven ten days thereafter. Women begin preparing a month before the festival, weaving intricate decorations from coconut-palm leaves, baking festive rice cakes and stockpiling packets of incense.

Towering bamboo poles are erected outside every gate, turning simple lanes into avenues of magnificently decorated *penjor*—looped scrolls of coconut leaf, decorated with vividly coloured leaves and tied with sheaves of rice and pieces of fabric, with intricate weavings of young coconut leaf and flowers dangling at the ends.

The day before Galungan is devoted to preparing festive dishes. Embossed silver or aluminium plates are readied with pieces of sugar cane, betel leaf, several types of rice cake, and a few grains of cooked rice and dried beans in a small tray made

from a palm leaf. Fragrant trays of brilliant flowers, shredded leaves soaked in perfume and sticks of incense are also prepared. Every item of ritual significance is then placed precisely according to the rules of tradition.

On the morning of the big day, every Balinese wears exquisite traditional clothes. Women, carrying offering trays balanced on their heads, appear like flocks of brilliant tropical birds, their bodies wrapped in tightly wound sarongs and *kebayas* (blouses) of cerise, scarlet, emerald, sapphire green, gold or purple lace.

Offerings on the move. Strength of belief requires not only spiritual fortitude in Bali.

With the offerings made at the family shrines, married women then attend to the shrines at the homes of their parents. After the offerings and the feasting, the children have fun prowling the streets with gongs, drums and a *barong* (a mythological beast considered protector of the village) with a couple of dancers inside. Families crowd into the lanes to be entertained. With the spirits feted and all mortals well-fed and content, balance and harmony is maintained throughout the island.

Snacking as a Way of Life

*Fast food Bali-style is an essential
part of the daily diet*

Although they eat meals only twice a day, the Balinese are always snacking. Women rush from the family compound into the street the minute a passing food vendor twangs the metal chime on his push cart; men stop off at their local *warung* shop for a coffee and on the way home from the padi fields, while school children cannot resist crisp fried crackers (*krupuk*) or a plate of *rujak*, sliced sour fruit with a sweet and pungent sauce.

*An abundance
of snacks at a
Balinese market.*

The *warung* is more than just a place to have a snack, buy a packet of clove-scented *kretek* cigarettes, a box of mosquito coils or a small bag of washing powder, it is somewhere to meet friends, and a major focal point of the village. Often with walls of plaited bamboo strips and a packed dirt or cement floor, most *warung* consist simply of a large table crammed with merchandise, and a long wooden bench set in front.

Lined up along the front of the table are bottles of local soft drink, beer and plastic bottles of mineral water. Among the confusing and colourful jumble of enamelled basins piled with packets, screw-top plastic jars, bunches of bananas and perhaps a pile of fruits for making *rujak,* there are innumerable options for a quick snack: salted peanuts, huge savoury *rempeyek* or rice-flour biscuits with peanuts, all kinds of biscuits and cakes, sweet bread rolls, candies and *krupuk.*

Rickety looking stalls, little more than a simple cart on bicycle wheels, painted in primary colours, with a plastic or glass display case on top, are found everywhere in Bali. Generally operated by non-Balinese, these mobile food stalls do a roaring trade serving just one dish. *Mie bakso* (meat-ball and noodle soup), *tauhu goreng* (deep-fried stuffed beancurd), boiled mung beans in a sweet sauce and brightly coloured concoctions of syrup and fruits are favourites provided by the mobile vendors.

Most markets have a cluster of very rudimentary food stalls consisting of a trestle table, benches and a plastic canopy to provide some shade. Market foodstalls generally offer non-Balinese food: popular items are noodle soups such as *soto Madura*, Javanese-style *sate* and *murtabak*, fried savoury pancakes that are Indian in origin.

If you're fortunate, there may be a stall selling a range of Balinese food; ask for *nasi campur* (literally mixed rice) and you'll be given a bowl of rice with perhaps a few shreds of fried chicken, a leaf-wrapped bundle of finely chopped seasonings and meat, some steamed vegetables with shredded savoury coconut, fried peanuts, a ladleful of coconut milk gravy, a sprinkle of crisp-fried shallots and a dollop of spicey hot ground chilli paste (*sambal*).

On market days in smaller villages, or daily in major towns, there's sure to be a stall selling the ever-popular *be guling celeng*, better known by its Indonesian name, *babi guling*. Order a plate of this and you'll get a little succulent spit-roasted pork; slices of a couple of types of sausage made with the intestines stuffed with finely chopped pieces of highly seasoned meat; some spiced coconut milk gravy; *lawar*, a complex mixture of seasonings, steamed vegetable and a little raw pounded pork and pig's blood, and a couple of crisp pieces of pork crackling made from the skin. All this goes with

Priests enjoy a meal within the temple grounds during a festival.

steamed rice and often a vegetable dish made from young jackfruit or *nangka*.

The Balinese aren't likely to be surprised to see tourists stopping to snack at a *warung*, to have a bowl of noodles from a pushcart or to enjoy a quick meal in the market. After all, everyone's got to eat and even foreigners can't be expected to wait for several hours until the next meal without having a little something to keep them going.

Part Two: The Balinese Kitchen

Simple yet sophisticated cooking: a practical
marriage of ancient and modern

Despite the complex blending of spices and fragrant roots that gives Balinese food its intriguingly different flavour, the typical Balinese kitchen is remarkably simple. The centrepiece of the kitchen—generally a spartan, functional room—is the wood-fired stove topped by a blackened clay pot used to steam rice and leaf-wrapped food. In many modern households, this is joined by a gas cooker for boiling water and frying. Both stoves receive daily offerings of a few grains of rice, a flower and salt—a gift to Brahma, the animistic god of fire.

Although all utensils were once made of clay, most cooks now use metal for cooking. Many people in the major towns also use electric rice cookers, but most agree that the traditional method for cooking rice is superior. After the rice has been well washed and soaked, it is partially boiled then set in a woven steaming basket (*kukusan*) over a clay pot filled with boiling water. The conical *kukusan* is covered with a clay lid and the rice left to steam. Every so often, boiling water is scooped out of the clay pot and poured over the rice to keep it moist and prevent the grains from sticking together.

Bamboo is often used in the Balinese kitchen. A narrow bamboo tube is used to direct a puff of air into the fire, acting as a bellows. A split length of bamboo plaited so that it fans out is used as a scoop for lifting out and draining fried food, while bamboo handles with small coconut shells on the end make scoops or ladles.

Every Balinese kitchen has its coconut scraper, either a wooden board set with rows of sharp metal spikes or a sheet of thin aluminium with spikes punched out. Grated coconut is mixed into many dishes, or squeezed with water to make coconut milk.

Another essential item is the saucer-like stone mortar (*batu base*) used for grinding dry spices, chillies, shallots and other seasonings. The Balinese mortar is shallow and the stone pestle has a handle carved at right-angles to the head so that the action is one of grinding rather than pounding.

The chopping block used in the preparation of almost every meal is usually a cross-section slice of a tree trunk, the wood strong enough to take the repeated blows of a sharp cleaver used to mince meat or fish to a paste, and for chopping and slicing various roots and vegetables.

The furniture in a Balinese kitchen is minimal; apart from the stove, a bench and a food cupboard, where the cooked food is stored during the day, there's usually a wide, low bamboo platform, used for sitting on while preparing foods. It also doubles as an eating area, or a spare bed. Practicality is the theme of any Balinese kitchen.

Basic Equipment

A few simple tools and utensils

Preparing Balinese food abroad does not require an excess of complex equipment, and with the increasing popularity of Asian cuisines around the world, basic ingredients are generally easy to obtain.

One important item you'll need is a solid **wooden chopping block** (the bigger the better) and a heavy **cleaver**. This versatile item does everything from chopping up a whole chicken to mincing meat and seafood, bruising a stalk of lemon grass to smashing cardamom pods so they release their fragrance; it is also used to finely chop the chillies, shallots and fragrant roots for seasoning.

Balinese cooks prefer to use terracotta or clay pots, although these are increasingly being augmented by metal pans. **Stainless steel** or **enamelled pans** are recommended as the acidity in many dishes makes the use of aluminium inadvisable.

Wooden Balinese rice scoops.

The classic method of cooking rice in Bali is to steam it in a cone of woven bamboo which is inserted over a clay pot of boiling water. Many modern cooks, however, are now turning to **electric rice cookers**, which not only ensure perfectly cooked rice every time but also keep cooked rice warm. A heavy pot with a firm-fitting lid is a suitable substitute.

For stir-frying rice and noodles, and for deep frying, nothing beats the **wok**. Its shape means that food tossed during stir frying falls back in the pan and not outside, and less oil is required than a conventional pan for deep frying. In Bali the wok is also used for braised dishes.

The simplest way of **steaming** wrapped bundles of food—a popular Balinese cooking method—is to place it on a perforated metal disc that sits inside a wok, a few centimetres above boiling water, the wok covered with a domed lid. If you don't have a wok, food can be placed in the steaming basket of a pressure cooker, but be sure not to use the valve on the lid during steaming.

Every Balinese kitchen has a mortar and pestle, used for crushing spices and for making a coarse paste of shallots, chillies and fragrant roots. There's quite a knack in using the shallow grinding stone favoured by the Balinese, and in most cases, a **food processor** with a small bowl or a powerful blender will do the job adequately.

Banana leaves are indispensible to the Balinese cook for wrapping food for steaming, grilling and roasting. The leaf is wiped clean, then softened either in a fire (a gas flame is ideal) or in boiling water before being wrapped around the food. **Aluminium foil** can be substituted, but it lacks the moisture and subtle flavor imparted by the banana leaf.

TUM WRAPPING

Step 1: *place ingredients in centre of clean leaf and pleat in side as shown*

Step 2: *repeat on other side*

Step 3: *fold one end of pleat to the front and the other to the back*

Step 4: *repeat on other side to firmly enclose contents*

Step 5: *put bundle in centre of strip of leaf and fold up to hold the pleats together*

Step 6: *secure with a toothpick*

GRILLED FISH IN BANANA LEAF

Step 1: *place ingredients along the piece of clean leaf as shown*

Step 2: *roll over firmly*

Step 3: *secure both ends of the roll with toothpicks*

Cooking Methods

*Subtleties are vital for the creation of
authentic-tasting Balinese dishes*

Balinese cooking methods are similar to those employed in any other Asian or Western kitchen, although there are differences that should be noted.

Blanching is often used for vegetables, as well as for bones to make stock. To blanch vegetables, bring a large amount of water with 2 teaspoons of salt to every 4 cups of liquid to a rapid boil in a large heavy stock pot. Add the vegetables and bring back to a rapid boil; cook uncovered for just 1 minute. Drain vegetables thoroughly. Although Balinese cooks don't do so, you'll improve the colour and texture of the vegetables by plunging them in ice water for a couple of minutes to cool. Drain and dry.

A clay rice bowl.

When **boiling** vegetables or meat, use a heavy pot and bring liquid to a rapid boil. Add food and simmer with the pot uncovered until tender.

Steaming should be done over boiling water, using either a rack set inside a wok, a basket set inside a pressure cooker (without valve), or a rack set well above the water level inside a large saucepan. Bring water to the boil, add the food, cover and reduce heat slightly to ensure the water keeps boiling. Replenish the water as it evaporates.

Braising is often done in a wok in Bali. Meat or seafood are first sealed in oil over high heat; spices or seasonings are added and then the liquid. This is brought to the boil, the heat reduced, the wok covered and the food simmered until cooked. Turn the meat frequently during cooking and add more stock or liquid if necessary. If there is too much liquid, reduce it by removing the lid and increasing heat.

Extremely high heat is required for **stir frying**. The wok should be heated before the addition of oil; when the oil begins to smoke lightly, add the ingredients and fry, stirring constantly, until the dish is cooked. When **deep frying**, heat the oil in a wok, heavy pan or deep fryer. Add the food a little at a time so that the temperature will not drop, causing the food to absorb too much oil and become soggy.

Roasting in Bali is a time-consuming process. Food placed in a covered clay pot is set over a slow fire. Use a gas or electric oven and a heavy roasting pan, which should be heated before the food is added. Baste frequently during cooking.

Charcoal grilling is used mainly for satay. The food is first marinated with spices and left for up to 24 hours. Start the fire at least one hour in advance. While the food is grilling, use a hand fan to keep the coals glowing: the Balinese always slightly char their barbecued food. The favourite fuel in Bali is made from coconut husks, but charcoal can be substituted.

Preparing Rice

*In Bali, a meal is not a meal without rice,
a subject which arouses passions*

Steamed or boiled rice, the staple food in Bali, is the centrepiece of every main meal. Leftover rice is often transformed and reappears as *Nasi Goreng*, fried with various savoury ingredients. In addition, various types of rice are used in desserts and cakes, either whole or ground into flour,

The subject of rice can arouse passions among the Balinese, who grow the fast-growing, disease-resistant modern strains as a commercial crop but are prepared to pay up to four times more to buy traditional varieties which are deemed to have infinitely more flavour.

For most meals, **long-grain white rice** is used; the fragrant Thai varieties available in the West are probably the closest in taste to good Balinese rice. For desserts and cakes, two types of **glutinous rice** are used: one is dark brownish-black in colour (*injin*) and the other a cloudy white (*ketan*). Finely ground white rice or **rice flour** is also used for cakes and desserts.

Rice should always be thoroughly washed before cooking, as any starch clinging to the outside of the grain will cause the rice to become soggy. A rice cooker produces excellent results, and is favoured by an increasing number of modern Balinese cooks.

In the absence of the rice cooker, use a heavy pan with a firm-fitting lid with the following method.

PLAIN RICE (*NASI PUTIH*)

To cook rice by the absorption method, which obtains a similar result to the steaming traditionally employed by the Balinese, wash $1\frac{1}{2}$ cups of long-grain rice until the water runs off clean. Put together with an equal amount of water in a heavy pan. Cover and bring to the boil over high heat. Stir once, lower heat and cook over moderate heat until all the water is absorbed. Stir the rice with a fork to fluff it up, cover the pan and remove from the heat for about 10 minutes to allow the rice to dry.

A traditional rice steamer.

COCONUT RICE (*NASI GURIH*)

Another popular method of cooking rice. Wash $1\frac{1}{2}$ cups of rice thoroughly and put in a pan with $2\frac{1}{2}$ cups thick coconut milk, 1 *pandan* leaf, 2 *salam* leaves and 1 teaspoon of salt. Cover the pan and bring to the boil over moderate heat. Continue to cook until all the liquid is absorbed, stirring two or three times. Take care to keep the temperature moderate so that the rice does not burn. When the rice is cooked, remove it from the heat for 10 minutes.

The Balinese Cupboard

1	**7**	**13**		**24**	**29**		**40**
	8				**30**	**36**	**41**
2	**9**	**14**	**19**	**25**	**31**	**37**	**42**
3	**10**	**15**	**20**	**26**	**32**		**43**
4	**11**	**16**	**21**	**27**	**33**	**38**	**44**
5		**17**	**22**		**34**		**45**
6	**12**	**18**	**23**	**28**	**35**	**39**	

1 lemon grass
2 *krupuk kedele*
3 tamarind pulp
4 plain white rice
5 *pandan* leaf
6 salt
7 *krupuk melinjo*
8 nutmeg
9 garlic
10 kaffir lime
11 cinnamon
12 cardamom
13 plain white rice
14 *kencur*
15 turmeric
16 bird's-eye chillies
17 *tabia Bali* chillies

18 black shrimp paste
19 ginger
20 *laos*
21 glutinous black rice
22 fragrant lime leaf
23 glutinous white rice
24 thin-skinned lime
25 soya sauce
26 white peppercorns
27 grated coconut
28 red rice
29 *krupuk ikan*
30 shallots
31 coriander seeds
32 *salam* leaf

33 black peppercorns
34 *krupuk bawang*
35 peanuts
36 cloves
37 *krupuk ikan*
38 candle nuts
39 *tabia lombok* chillies
40 *rempeyek*
41 fresh coconut
42 green *tabia lombok* chillies
43 palm sugar
44 lemon basil
45 dried shrimp paste

Balinese Ingredients

*An array of items ranging from
the familiar to the exotic*

Balinese food uses a number of ingredients already familiar to lovers of other Asian cuisines. These and other less familiar seasonings are described for easy identification, and a range of substitutes suggested. Names given in italics are Balinese or Indonesian.

LEMON BASIL (*don kemangi*): a fragrant, lemon-scented herb added at the last minute to keep its flavour, or used as a garnish. Although the flavour will be different, you can use another type of basil.

CANDLENUT (*tingkih*): a round, cream coloured nut with an oily consistency used to add texture and a faint flavour to many dishes. Substitutes: macadamia nuts or raw cashews.

CARDAMOM (*kepulaga*): a straw-coloured, fibrous pod encloses pungent black seeds. Each pod contains about 8-12 seeds; try to buy the whole pod rather than a jar of seeds as the flavour is more intense.

CHILLIES: three types of chilli pepper are used in Bali, with the amount of heat increasing as the size diminishes. Mildest and least popular are the finger-length red chillies (*tabia lombok*), usually seeded before use. The most commonly used is the short, fat *tabia Bali*, about 2.5 cm (1 in) long and ranging in colour from yellow to red. Hottest of all are the tiny fiery bird's-eye chillies (*tabia kerinyi*). The Balinese often mix green or unripe bird's-eye chilli together with the ripe red ones, as the flavour is less important than the intense heat they provide. Use only fresh and not dried chillies, and be careful to wash your hands thoroughly after handling chillies as the oil can burn your eyes and skin. You may even like to wear rubber gloves.

The recipes in this book were prepared using the *tabia Bali*; if you do not like your food too spicy, reduce the amount of chillies suggested.

CINNAMON (*kayu manis*): the thick, dark brown bark of a type of cassia is used in Bali, rather than true cinnamon. The latter is far more subtle in flavour, and also considerably more expensive. Look for the bark rather than ground cinnamon.

CLOVES (*cengkeh*): this small, brown, nail-shaped spice was once found only in the islands of the Moluccas, east of Bali. Apart from its use as a flavouring in a number of Balinese dishes, it is used to make the clove-scented cigarettes that are popular throughout Indonesia.

COCONUT (*nguh*): coconuts are widely used in Bali, for making sugar, alcohol, housing, utensils, temple offerings and charcoal. The grated flesh of the coconut is frequently added to food; it can also be squeezed in water to make coconut milk. If freshly grated coconut is not available, dessicated coconut moistened with warm water can be used as a substitute.

To make **fresh coconut milk**, put 2 cups of freshly grated ripe coconut into a bowl and add 2 cups of lukewarm water. Squeeze and knead the coconut thoroughly for 1 minute, then strain through cheesecloth into a bowl to obtain thick coconut milk. Repeat the process with another 1 cup of water to obtain thin coconut milk. Combine both lots of milk for the coconut milk called for in recipes in this book. Coconut milk can be deep frozen; thaw and stir thoroughly before use.

A distinctive Balinese flavour is obtained by roasting chunks of fresh coconut in a charcoal fire until blackened on all sides. The charred exterior is then brushed off, the flesh grated and coconut milk made in the normal way to obtain **roasted coconut milk**.

The best substitute for fresh coconut milk to be used with vegetables, seafood, meat and for sauces is **instant coconut powder**. Combine this with warm water as directed on the packet. For the richer, creamier flavour required for desserts and cakes, use **tinned coconut cream**.

CORIANDER SEEDS (*ketumbar*): small straw-coloured seeds with a faintly orange flavour. Whole seeds are usually lightly crushed before use.

GARLIC (*kesuna*): recipes in this book were prepared with Balinese garlic, the cloves of which are considerably smaller and less pungent than the garlic found in many Western countries. Adjust the amount to suit your taste, although bear in mind that the garlic is important to Balinese dishes.

GINGER (*jahe*): this pale creamy yellow root is widely used in Balinese cooking. Always scrape the skin off fresh ginger before using, and never substitute powdered ginger as the taste is quite different. Ginger can be stored in a cool place for several weeks.

KENCUR (*cekuh*): sometimes known as lesser galangal, the botanical name of this ginger-like root is *Kaemferia galanga*. It has a unique, pungent flavour and should be used sparingly. Wash it and, if you're fussy (most Balinese cooks aren't) scrape off the skin before using.

Dried sliced *kencur* or *kencur* powder can be used as a substitute. Soak dried slices in boiling water for 30 minutes; use $^1/_2$–1 teaspoon of powder for 2.5 cm (1 in) fresh root.

" SAR KEONG "

KRUPUK: dried crackers made from shrimps, fish, vegetables or nuts mixed with various types of flour are used as a garnish or eaten as a snack in Bali. They must be thoroughly dry before deep frying in very hot oil for a few seconds, so that they puff up and become crisp.

LAOS (*isen*): sometimes called galangal, this member of the ginger family has a very tough but elusively scented root which must be peeled before use. Substitute slices of dried *laos* (soaked in boiling water for 30 minutes) or powdered *laos* (1 teaspoon = 2.5 cm / 1 in).

LEMON GRASS (*sereh*): this intensely fragrant herb is used to impart a lemony flavour to soups, seafood and meat dishes and spice pastes. It can also be used as a skewer for satays. Cut off the roots and peel off the hard outer leaves; use only the tender bottom portion (15-20 cm / 6–8 in). If the lemon grass is not required sliced, it is normally hit a couple of times with the edge of a cleaver or a pestle to release the fragrance, and tied in a knot to hold it together during cooking.

LIME: three types of lime are encountered in Bali. The most popular and also the most fragrant is the leprous or **Kaffir lime** (*lemo*); the double leaf of this lime (*don lemo*) is often very finely shredded and added to minced fish, or left whole and added to food cooked in liquid. Use kitchen scissors to ensure that the leaf is cut into hair-like shreds. If fragrant lime leaf is not available, use the zest of a lime or lemon.

Lime juice from the Kaffir lime was used for recipes in this book; however, the milder juice of a small round **thin-skinned lime** (*juwuk lengis*) is also used in Bali, as elsewhere in Southeast Asia.

A large lime similar to those found internationally grows in Bali, and makes an acceptable substitute for the Kaffir lime; if limes are not available, use lemon juice.

NUTMEG (*jebog garum*): always grate whole nutmeg just before using as the powdered spice quickly loses its fragrance.

PALM SUGAR (*gula Bali*): juice extracted from the coconut flower or *aren* palm is boiled and packed into moulds to make sugar with a faint caramel taste. If palm sugar is not available, substitute soft brown sugar.

To make **palm sugar syrup**, combine 2 cups of chopped palm sugar with 1 cup of water and 2 pandan leaves. Bring to boil, simmer 10 minutes, strain and store in refrigerator.

PANDAN LEAF (*don pandan*): the fragrant leaf of a type of pandanus sometimes known as fragrant screwpine, this is tied in a knot and used to flavour desserts and cakes.

PEANUTS (*kacang tanah*): used raw and ground to make sauce, or deep fried and used as a garnish or condiment.

PEPPER (*merica*): both black and white peppercorns are crushed just before use; ground white pepper powder is also used on occasion.

SALAM LEAF (*don jangan ulam*): a subtly flavoured leaf of the cassia family, this bears no resemblance whatsoever to the taste of a bay leaf, which is sometimes suggested as a substitute. If you cannot obtain dried *salam* leaf, omit altogether.

SHALLOTS (*bawang barak*): widely used in Balinese cooking, pounded up to make spice pastes, sliced and added to food before cooking, and sliced and deep fried to make a garnish.

Balinese shallots are smaller and milder than those found in many Western countries, so you may need to reduce the amount called for in these recipes, which were prepared using Balinese shallots.

SHRIMP PASTE, DRIED (*trasi*): this very pungent seasoning often smells offensive to Westerners at first; it is always cooked before eating, generally toasted over a fire before being combined with other ingredients.

The best way to treat it is to spread the required amount on a piece of foil and to toast it under a grill for a minute or so on each side. Widely known overseas by its Indonesian name, *trasi*, or the Malay term, *belacan*, shrimp paste ranges in colour from purplish pink to brownish black, and is generally sold in a cake.

SHRIMP PASTE, BLACK (*petis*): a very thick syrupy paste with a strong shrimp flavour used in some sauces.

SOYA SAUCE: two types of soya sauce are used: thick **sweet soya sauce** (*kecap manis*), and the thinner, more salty thin **soya sauce** (*kecap asin*). If you cannot obtain *kecap manis*, use the dark black Chinese soya sauce and add brown sugar to sweeten it.

TAMARIND (*lunak*): the dark brown pod of the tamarind tree contains a sour fleshy pulp which adds a fruity sourness to many dishes. Packets of pulp usually contain the seeds and fibres.

To make **tamarind juice**, measure the pulp and soak it in hot water for 5 minutes before squeezing it to extract the juice, discarding the seeds, fibre and any skin.

TURMERIC (*kunyit*): a vivid yellow root of the ginger family, this has a very emphatic flavour. Scrape the skin before using. If fresh turmeric is not available, substitute 1 teaspoon of powdered turmeric for 2.5 cm/1 in of the fresh root.

To make **turmeric water**, peel about 20 cm (8 in) of fresh turmeric root; slice finely and combine with 1 cup of water. Process in a blender until very fine, or pound the sliced turmeric in a mortar and then mix with water and let stand for a couple of minutes. Strain through a sieve, pressing firmly with the back of a spoon to extract all the juice. Store in a jar in the refrigerator.

If fresh turmeric is not available, combine 4 tablespoons of powdered turmeric with 1 cup of water and mix well.

Part Three: The Recipes

Basic recipes for spice pastes, sauces, stocks and condiments precede those for the dishes, which begin on page 48

As in almost all of Asia, food is seldom served in individual portions in Bali. As a general rule, the following recipes will serve 4–6 people as part of a meal with rice and three other dishes.

BASE • SPICE PASTES

These basic spice pastes can be stored in a refrigerator for up to a week. They can also be divided into smaller quantities and deep frozen.

If you are using a mortar and pestle, grind the dry spices first; then add the hardest ingredients such as *laos* and *kencur,* before adding shallots, chillies, and other soft ingredients. If using a food processor, blend the dry spices first then add all other ingredients, except the oil.

Base Gede • *Basic Spice Paste*

This basic marinade is used mainly to neutralise the strong flavour of duck, lamb or pork, and also for turtle. Makes about 2 cups.

25 shallots, peeled and chopped
12 cloves garlic, peeled and chopped
7 large red chillies, seeded and chopped
5 cm (2 in) *laos*, peeled and chopped
5 cm (2 in) *kencur* root, peeled and chopped
10 cm (4 in) fresh turmeric, peeled and chopped

Measurements

Measurements in this book are given in volume as far as possible: 1 measuring **cup** contains 250 ml (roughly 8 oz); 1 **teaspoon** contains 5 ml, while 1 **tablespoon** contains 15 ml or the equivalent of 3 teaspoons. Australian readers please note that the standard Australian measuring spoon is larger, containing 20 ml or 4 teaspoons, so use only ¾ tablespoon when following the recipes. Where metric measurements are given, approximate imperial conversions follow in brackets.

Time Estimates

Time estimates for preparation only (excluding cooking) are based on the assumption that a food processor or blender will be used.

🕐 *quick and very easy to prepare*

🕐🕐 *relatively easy; less than 15 minutes preparation*

🕐🕐🕐 *takes more than 15 minutes to prepare*

Pages 38–39:
A sumptuous spread of Balinese dishes.
Opposite:
Grinding the basic spice paste, the starting point of any dish.

1 tablespoon coriander seeds
6 candlenuts
2 teaspoons dried shrimp paste
$^1/_2$ teaspoon black peppercorns
1 pinch freshly grated nutmeg
3 cloves
4 tablespoons oil

Pound or process all ingredients except oil according to the method given above. Heat oil in wok or heavy pan, add all ingredients and cook over high heat, stirring frequently, for 5 minutes until the marinade turns golden. Cool before using.

Base be Siap • *Spice Paste for Chicken*

Opposite:
Base Be Pasih,
*the basic
seasoning for
many seafood
dishes.*

14 shallots, peeled
26 cloves garlic, peeled
2.5 cm (1 in) *kencur* root, peeled and chopped
4 cm (1$^1/_2$ in) *laos*, peeled and chopped
10 candlenuts
12 cm (5 in) fresh turmeric, peeled and
  chopped
4 tablespoons chopped palm sugar
4 tablespoons vegetable oil
2 stalks lemon grass, bruised
2 *salam* leaves
10 bird's-eye chillies, finely sliced

Put shallots, garlic, *kencur, laos,* candlenuts, turmeric and palm sugar into a food processor and grind coarsely. Heat oil and fry all ingredients until very hot, stirring frequently, until the marinade changes to a golden colour. Cool before using.

Base be Sampi • *Spice Paste for Beef*

To maximise the flavour of meat, make sure it is thoroughly coated with this marinade and refrigerate for 24 hours before using.

10 shallots, peeled and chopped
6 cloves garlic, peeled and chopped
5 cm (2 in) ginger, peeled and chopped
10 cm (4 in) *laos*, peeled and chopped
6 large red chillies, seeded and chopped
7 bird's-eye chillies
10 candlenuts
1 tablespoon coriander seeds
1 tablespoon black peppercorns
2 *salam* leaves
4 tablespoons chopped palm sugar
4 tablespoons oil

Combine all ingredients except *salam* leaves and oil, place in food processor and grind coarsely. Heat vegetable oil in heavy saucepan or wok until very hot. Add ground ingredients together with *salam* leaves and cook over medium heat for 5 minutes, stirring frequently, until marinade changes to golden colour. Set aside and cool before using.

Base be Pasih • *Spice Paste for Seafood*

10 large red chillies, seeded and chopped
6 cloves garlic, peeled and chopped
15 shallots, peeled and chopped
10 cm (4 in) ginger, peeled and chopped
10 cm (4 in) fresh turmeric, peeled and
  chopped
1 medium-sized tomato, skinned and seeded
1 tablespoon coriander seeds
10 candlenuts
1 teaspoon dried shrimp paste
4 tablespoons oil
3 tablespoons tamarind pulp
2 *salam* leaves
2 stalks lemon grass

Process all ingredients except oil, tamarind pulp, *salam* leaves and lemon grass until coarsely ground.

Heat oil, add all ingredients and cook over moderate heat for about 5 minutes, stirring frequently, until golden. Cool before using.

Base Jukut • *Spice Paste for Vegetables*

8 shallots, peeled and chopped
10 cloves garlic, peeled and chopped
30 cm (12 in) *laos*, peeled and thinly sliced
1 teaspoon coriander seeds
10 cm (4 in) fresh turmeric, peeled and sliced
6 large red chillies, seeded and chopped
3–5 bird's-eye chillies
5 cm (2 in) *kencur* roots, peeled and chopped
1 teaspoon dried shrimp paste
2 tablespoons oil
1 teaspoon salt
1/4 teaspoon ground white pepper
1 *salam* leaf, whole
1 stalk lemon grass, bruised

Place shallots, garlic, *laos*, coriander seeds, turmeric, chillies, *kencur* and dried shrimp paste in food processor and purée lightly, or grind coarsely in mortar. Heat oil in wok or heavy saucepan. Add the ground paste and remaining ingredients, and sauté for 2 minutes or until marinade changes colour. Cool before using.

SAMBALS

Sambel Tomat • *Tomato Sambal*

4 tablespoons oil
15 shallots, peeled and sliced
10 cloves garlic, peeled and sliced
14 large red chillies, seeds removed, sliced
2 medium-sized tomatoes each cut in 6 wedges

2 teaspoons roasted dried shrimp paste
2 teaspoons freshly squeezed lime juice

Heat oil in a heavy saucepan or wok. Add shallots and garlic and saute 5 minutes over low heat. Add chillies and sauté another 5 minutes, then add tomato and shrimp paste and simmer for another 10 minutes.

Add lime juice. Put all ingredients in a food procesor and puree coarsely. Season to taste with salt. Cool before using. This sambal can be deep frozen. An ideal accompaniment to grilled fish.

Sambel Sere Tabia • *Fried Bird's-Eye Chillies*

Clean and discard the stems of about **25 bird's-eye chillies**. Heat **1/4 cup oil** in a wok or saucepan until smoking hot. Crumble **1 1/2 teaspoons dried shrimp paste** and combine with **1/4 teaspoon salt**.

Add chillies, shrimp paste and salt to the oil, stir over heat for 1 minute and then remove from heat and allow to cool. Store chillies and cooking oil in an airtight container for up to 1 week in a refrigerator.

Sambel Matah • *Shallot & Lemon Grass Sambal*

15 shallots
4 cloves garlic, sliced finely
10–15 bird's-eye chillies, sliced
5 fragrant lime leaves, cut in hair-like shreds
1 teaspoon roasted dried shrimp paste
4 stalks lemon grass, tender part only, very finely sliced
1 teaspoon salt
1/4 teaspoon black peppercorns, finely crushed
2 tablespooons freshly squeezed lime juice
1/3 cup oil

Peel shallots and slice in half lengthwise, then cut in fine crosswise slices. Combine with all other ingredients and mix thoroughly for a couple of minutes before serving with fish or chicken.

SAUCES

Base Satay • *Satay Sauce*

500 g (1 lb) raw peanuts, deep fried for 2 minutes
5 cloves garlic, peeled
6–10 bird's-eye chillies
10 cm (4 in) kencur root, peeled and chopped
$^1/_2$ cup chopped palm sugar
2 litres (8 cups) fresh coconut milk
4 tablespoons sweet soya sauce
1 tablespoon freshly squeezed lime juice
1 tablespoon fried shallots

Combine peanuts, garlic, chillies and kencur in a food processor and puree, or grind coarsely in a stone mortar. Put in heavy pan with coconut milk and sweet soya sauce.

Bring to a boil, reduce heat and simmer uncovered, stirring frequently to prevent the sauce from sticking, for 1 hour. Add lime juice and sprinkle with shallots just before serving as a dipping sauce for satay.

Base Rujak • *Rujak Sauce*

6 tablespoons tamarind pulp
1 cup palm sugar syrup (page 36)
1 teaspoon dried shrimp paste, roasted
6 bird's-eye chillies, left whole
$^1/_2$ teaspoon salt
$^1/_2$ cup water

Combine all ingredients in a heavy pan and bring slowly to the boil. Stir well and simmer for 10 minutes. When cool, squeeze to extract all the juice from the tamarind and strain through a sieve.

Base Kacang • *Peanut Sauce*

500g (1 lb) raw peanuts, deep fried for 2 minutes
4 cloves garlic, peeled
10-15 bird's-eye chillies, sliced
3 fragrant lime leaves
$^1/_2$ cup sweet soya sauce
2 tablespoons fried shallots
8 cm (3 in) *kencur* root, peeled and coarsely chopped
1 tablespoon freshly squeezed lime juice
2 teaspoons salt
1.5 litres (6 cups) water

Combine peanuts, garlic, *kencur* and chillies and process or grind until coarse. Put in a heavy pan with all other ingredients except lime juice and shallots and simmer over very low heat for 1 hour, stirring constantly to prevent the sauce from burning. Stir in lime juice and sprinkle with shallots just before serving.

STOCK

Kuah Siap • *Chicken Stock*

5 kg (11 lb) chicken bones, chopped in 2.5 cm (1 in) pieces
$1^1/_2$ cups chicken spice paste
1 stalk lemon grass, lightly bruised
3 fragrant lime leaves
2 *salam* leaves

**1 teaspoon black peppercorns, coarsely
crushed
1 teaspoon salt**

Rinse bones until water is clear, put in large saucepan with cold water to cover and bring to boil. Drain water, wash bones again under running water. Return bones to the pan, cover with fresh water and return to the boil. Reduce heat and remove scum with a ladle.

Add all seasoning ingredients and simmer stock gently for 3-3½ hours, removing scum as it accumulates. Do not cover the pan during cooking as it will make the stock cloudy. Strain stock, cool and store in small containers in the deep freezer. To make **beef**, **duck** and **pork** stock, use the same quantities but reduce simmering time for pork to 2 hours. Makes 3 litres.

CONDIMENTS

Bawang Goreng • *Fried Shallots*

Peel and thinly slice 10–15 shallots. Dry on a paper towel. Heat about ¼ cup oil until moderately hot. Add shallots and fry until golden brown.

Remove and drain thoroughly before storing in airtight jar.

Acar • *Pickled Vegetables*

**1 small cucumber, cut in matchsticks
1 medium-sized carrot, cut in matchsticks
10-15 bird's-eye chillies
6 shallots, peeled and quartered
½ cup water**

**½ cup white sugar
½ cup distilled white vinegar
pinch of salt**

Combine water, sugar, vinegar and salt in a pan, bring to the boil, simmer one minute and then allow to cool. Mix vegetables with the dressing.

Refrigerate for at least 24 hours before serving at room temperature.

Saur • *Fried Shredded Coconut*

**1 cup finely grated fresh coconut, or
dessicated coconut, moistened with
warm water
2 tablespoons chicken spice paste
(page 42)
1½ tablespoons oil
1 tablespoon chopped palm sugar
a pinch of salt**

Combine coconut with spice paste. Heat oil in a wok, add coconut mixture and palm sugar and sauté over low heat until the coconut turns golden brown. Allow to cool before adding salt.

Stored in an airtight container it will keep fresh for several days.

Tabia Lalah Manis • *Chilli in Soya Sauce*

Slice **15 bird's-eye chillies** and mix with **¼ cup each** of **sweet soya sauce** (*kecap manis*) and **thin soya sauce** (*kecap asin*).

Do not store for any length of time as this sauce tends to turn soft and sour.

GEDANG MEKUAH

Green Papaya Soup

If you prefer to eat your papayas ripe and golden, you could try making this soup with any summer squash or Chinese winter melon instead. ⏱⏱

1 unripe papaya, weighing roughly 750 g (1½ lb)
1 cup vegetable spice paste (page 42)
1 litre (4 cups) chicken stock (page 46)
2 *salam* leaves
1 stalk lemon grass, bruised
¼ teaspoon powdered white pepper
1 teaspoon salt
fried shallots to garnish

Peel the papaya, cut in half lengthwise and remove the seeds. Slice the papaya lengthwise in 4 or 6 slices, then slice crosswise in slices about 0.5 cm (¼ in) thick.

Heat stock, add spice paste and chicken stock and bring to the boil. Simmer 2 minutes then add the *salam* leaves, lemon grass and papaya and simmer gently until the papaya is tender. If the stock reduces too much, add more. Season to taste with pepper and salt and garnish with fried shallots.

Helpful hints: To save time, you can use chicken stock cubes in place of home-made chicken stock although the taste will be nowhere near as good.

CRAM CAM

Clear Chicken Soup with Shallots

This dish is traditionally prepared after a cockfight, when the winner receives the losing chicken as a reward. ⏱ ⏱

l litre (4 cups) chicken stock (page 46)
¹/₂ cup chicken spice paste (page 42)
1 salam leaf
1 stalk lemon grass, bruised
400 g (13 oz) boneless chicken, skin removed and minced
salt to taste
1 teaspoon crushed black pepper
2 tablespoons fried shallots

Bring chicken stock to boil in stock pot. Wrap chicken spice paste and black pepper into piece of cotton cloth and tie with string. Add this together with the *salam* leaf and lemon grass to soup and simmer for 10 minutes.

Add minced chicken and continue to simmer for 15 minutes. Remove spice paste bundle from the soup and discard. Season soup to taste with salt and pepper and garnish with fried shallots.

Helpful hints*:* You can save time by buying minced or ground chicken. Wrapping the spice paste in a cloth will ensure that the soup is clear.

JUKUT ARES

Chicken Soup with Banana Stem

This soup is made from the centre of tender young banana plants that have not yet borne fruit; those from mature plants are used only as pig food in Bali. Don't worry if you are unable to get banana stem; you can use cabbage instead, but reduce the salting period to only 10 minutes. ⊘⊘

600 g (1¼ lb) young banana palm stem
6 tablespoons salt
½ cup basic spice paste (page 41)
1.5 litres (6 cups) chicken stock (page 46)
2 *salam* leaves
1 stalk lemon grass, bruised
salt to taste
½ teaspoon black peppercorns, crushed
fried shallots to garnish

Peel off hard outside layers of the banana stem, cut in half lengthwise and place flat side on carving board. With a sharp knife cut in thin slices. Sprinkle a flat tray with salt, place sliced banana stem on it and sprinkle generously with salt again. Marinate for 45 minutes. Place slices on top of each other and press by hand to extract the juice. Repeat process until stems are very dry and soft. Rinse stems thoroughly under running water. Strain and dry well.

Combine chicken stock and spice paste and bring to the boil. Add *salam* leaves and lemon grass. Simmer for 5 minutes then add shredded banana stem and bring back to boil. Simmer for one hour until stems are soft, but still crunchy. If using cabbage, the cooking time will be much shorter.

Season to taste with salt and pepper and garnish with fried shallots.

Helpful hints*:* Try replacing the chicken stock with home-made duck stock for a richer flavour.

SOTO BABAT
Clear Tripe Soup

This is usually served with *Sambel Tomat* as a contrasting condiment. The sugar cane is used to help soften the tripe rather than to add any sweetness to the soup; if this is not available, the cooking time will be slightly longer. ⏱ ⏱

600 g (1¼ lb) beef tripe, cleaned and washed well

3 litres (12 cups) water

1 litre (4 cups) beef stock (page 47)

5 cm (2 in) sugar cane stem, split lengthwise (optional)

2.5cm (1 in) ginger, peeled and sliced lengthwise

4 cloves garlic, peeled and sliced

1 tablespoon distilled white vinegar

200 g (6½ oz) giant white radish, peeled and diced in 1 cm (½ in) cubes

5 sprigs celery leaf, chopped

1 tablespoon fried shallots

Rinse tripe well under running water until very clean. Bring water to boil in a large pan, add tripe and simmer until soft (approximately 1 hour).

Strain water and cool tripe in ice water. Cut in pieces approximately 2.5 cm x 1cm (1 in x ½ in). Bring beef stock, sugar cane, ginger, garlic and vinegar to boil. Add tripe and radish. Simmer until vegetables are soft. Garnish with celery leaf and fried shallots.

Helpful hints*:* Any type of summer squash or Chinese winter melon can be used instead of giant white radish (Japanese *daikon*). This soup reheats well.

JUKUT KAKUL

Snail Soup

The French aren't the only ones to have a liking for snails. The Balinese gather snails in the rice fields, but you can use the canned variety. Cucumber, zucchini or any other summer squash can be used instead of green papaya. 🕐 🕐

   200 g (6½ oz) unripe green papaya
   1 litre (4 cups) chicken stock (page 46)
   ½ cup seafood spice paste (page 42)
   1 stalk lemon grass, bruised
   2 *salam* leaves
   1 tablespoon oil
   48 canned snails, washed and drained
   1 teaspoon salt
   freshly ground black pepper
   fried shallots to garnish

Peel the papaya, cut in half lengthwise and remove the seeds, then cut it lengthwise in 4 or 6 slices. Cut crosswise into slices about 0.5 cm (¼ in) thick. Combine stock, spice paste, lemon grass, *salam* leaves and oil in a large pot. Bring to the boil then simmer for 5 minutes. Add the papaya and simmer until almost tender. Add the snails and continue cooking until the papaya softens.

Season with salt and pepper to taste and garnish with fried shallots.

Helpful hints*:* If you do not care for snails, you can try using 12 dried black Chinese mushrooms, washed and soaked in warm water for 20 minutes, as a substitute. Add them together with the papaya to ensure they will be tender by the time the papaya is cooked.

URUTAN CELENG & CELENG ORET
Fried and Steamed Pork Sausages

URUTAN CELENG

These excellent spicy sausages are always found at food stalls selling roast pig (*Be Celeng* or *Babi Guling*) throughout Bali. ⏱ ⏱ ⏱

600 g (1¼ lb) boneless pork leg or shoulder, cut in 1cm (½ in) cubes
½ cup basic spice paste (page 41)
1 teaspoon salt
1 teaspoon black peppercorns, crushed
2 tablespoons tamarind pulp, seeds and fibres removed
vegetable oil for frying
1 metre (3 ft) pork intestine or sausage casings

Combine pork meat with basic spice paste, salt, pepper and tamarind paste. Mix well for 5 minutes. Tie one end of pork intestines with string. Insert large round nozzle into pastry piping bag and fill it with the meat mixture. Place open end of intestine over nozzle of piping bag and fill intestine tightly. Tie end with string. Dry sausage for 8 hours on wire rack in oven at very low heat. Deep fry in oil over medium heat until golden brown.

CELENG ORET ⏱ ⏱ ⏱

600 g (1¼ lb) minced pork
½ cup basic spice paste (page 41)
1 egg
1 teaspoon black peppercorns, crushed
2 tablespoons cornflour
2 tablespoons tamarind pulp, seeds and fibres removed
1 metre (3 ft) pork intestines

Follow same steps as for Urutan; however, this method does not require drying. Simply steam the sausage for 30 minutes or deep fry in moderately hot oil until golden brown.

Helpful hints*: The mixture can be formed into a 5 cm (2 in) roll, then wrapped in banana leaf or foil for steaming if you have difficulty obtaining sausage casings.*

BE CELENG BASE MANIS

Pork in Sweet Soya Sauce

This delicious sweet pork dish with a hint of ginger and plenty of chillies to spice it up often appears on festive occasions, when a whole pig is slaughtered and there's plenty of meat available. ⏱

2 tablespoons oil
5 shallots, peeled and sliced
5 cloves garlic, peeled and sliced
600 g (1¼ lb) boneless pork shoulder or leg, cut in 2 cm (¾ in) cubes
8 cm (3 in) ginger, peeled and sliced lengthwise
4 tablespoons sweet soya sauce
2 tablespoons thin soya sauce
1 teaspoon black peppercorns, crushed
2 cups chicken stock (page 46)
6–10 bird's-eye chillies, left whole

Heat oil in a wok or heavy saucepan. Add shallots and garlic and sauté for 2 minutes over medium heat or until lightly coloured. Add pork and ginger and continue to sauté for 2 more minutes over high heat. Add both lots of soya sauce and black pepper and continue sautéing for 1 minute.

Pour in chicken stock and simmer over medium heat for approximately 1 hour. When cooked, there should be very little sauce left and the meat should be shiny and dark brown. If the meat becomes too dry during cooking, add a little chicken stock.

Helpful hints*:* Some cooks like to pound the shallots, garlic and ginger together and fry them before adding the pork, making the resulting sauce thicker.

GULING CELENG

Suckling Pig

If there's just one dish that people remember after a visit to Bali, it's this famous delicacy, usually known by its Indonesian name, *Babi Guling*. ⏱ ⏱ ⏱

- 1 suckling pig, weighing about 6-8 kg (13–17 lb)
- 1¹⁄₂ tablespoons salt
- 10 shallots, peeled and sliced
- 6 cloves garlic, peeled and chopped
- 5 cm (2 in) ginger, peeled and chopped
- 15 candlenuts, chopped
- 10 cm (4 in) fresh turmeric, peeled and chopped
- 2 tablespoons coriander seeds, crushed
- 5 cm (2 in) *laos*, finely chopped
- 25–30 bird's-eye chillies, sliced
- 10 stalks lemon grass, sliced
- 1 tablespoon black peppercorns, crushed
- 1 teaspoon dried shrimp paste, roasted
- 5 fragrant lime leaves, finely shredded
- 2 *salam* leaves
- 2¹⁄₂ tablespoons oil
- 4 tablespoons turmeric juice (*see Balinese Ingredients*)

Ensure inside of suckling pig is completely cleaned out. Season inside and outside with salt.

Combine all other ingredients except turmeric juice and mix thoroughly. Fill inside of suckling pig with this mixture, close belly with string or thin satay skewer. Rub the outside of the pig with turmeric juice until the skin is shiny yellow.

Place suckling pig on roasting rack and roast in hot oven (200°C / 425°F) for approximately 1 hour. Rest for 10 minutes in warm place before serving. When serving, first remove the crisp skin with a strong carving knife, then loosen meat from the bones and cut into even dice or slices. Place a heaped tablespoon of stuffing on each serving plate, then top with meat and skin.

Traditionally this dish is eaten with Sayur Nangka and steamed rice.

Helpful hints: If you have a large barbecue with a rotisserie or constantly turning spit, you can cook the pig over charcoal for an authentic Balinese flavour.

KIKIL CELENG MEKUAH

Pork Knuckles in Spicy Sauce

The Balinese are very thrifty when it comes to food, but the wonderful melting texture of pig knuckes makes this dish more than just a practical way of ensuring that no part of the pig is wasted. ⏱

1.2 kg (2½ lb) pork knuckles, cut in
   2.5 cm (1 in) slices
2 tablespoons oil
8 shallots, peeled and chopped
3 cloves garlic, peeled and chopped
2.5 cm (1 in) ginger, peeled and chopped
2.5 cm (1 in) fresh turmeric, peeled
   and chopped
10 candlenuts, chopped
¾ teaspoon coriander seeds, crushed
2.5 cm (1 in) *kencur*, peeled and chopped
1 teaspoon dried shrimp paste
1 teaspoon black peppercorns, crushed
2 *salam* leaves
1 teaspoon salt
2 cups chicken stock
large red chillies, fried shallots
   and basil to garnish

Bring 3 litres (12 cups) of lightly salted water to boil in a stockpot. Add knuckles, reduce heat and simmer for approximately 45 minutes until meat is three quarter cooked.

Heat oil in heavy saucepan. Add all ingredients except chicken stock and sauté for about 2 minutes until spices change colour. Pour chicken stock into saucepan, mix well and bring to the boil. Add cooked knuckles, mix well, bring back to the boil, reduce heat and simmer for 10 minutes or until knuckles are completely cooked.

Garnish with sliced red chillies, fried shallots, and sprigs of fresh sliced lemon basil.

Helpful hints: If you cook this in advance and chill it, you will be able to remove some of the fat from the surface of the sauce.

BE SAMPI MESITSIT
Dry Spiced Beef

Don't be misled by the rather uninteresting appearance and name of this beef dish. It is wonderfully flavoured and generally so popular that it's worth making a large amount. Cook as directed below, then if you have leftovers after a meal, deep fry the beef until very crisp. Drain thoroughly and store in an airtight container. This crisp beef is excellent as a finger food with cocktails, and also makes a tasty accompaniment to rice-based meals. ☉☉☉

1 kg (2 lb) beef topside, cut in 4 steaks 250 g (8 oz) each
8 cloves garlic, peeled
2 teaspoons coriander seeds, crushed
1 tablespoon chopped palm sugar
2 large red chillies, seeded
2 tablespoons *laos*, peeled and sliced
2 teaspoons dried shrimp paste
2 cloves, ground
1 teaspoon salt
1 teaspoon black peppercorns, coarsely ground
2 tablespoons oil
2 teaspoons freshly squeezed lime juice

Bring 5 litres (20 cups) of lightly salted water to the boil in stockpot. Add beef and boil for approximately 1 hour until very tender. Remove from stock. Meat must be so tender that its fibres separate very easily. Keep stock. Pound meat until flat and shred by hand into fine fibres.

Place garlic, coriander, palm sugar, red chillies, *laos*, dried shrimp paste, cloves, salt and pepper in a food processor and puree coarsely, or grind in a stone mortar. Heat oil in heavy saucepan and sauté the marinade for 2 minutes over medium heat. Add shredded beef, mix well and sauté until dry. Season with lime juice.

Remove from heat and allow to cool. Serve at room temperature with steamed rice.

Helpful hints*:* Do not be tempted to use a food processor to shred the meat; you will obtain the correct texture only by shredding the meat with your fingers or a fork.

BE SAMPI MEBASE BALI

Braised Beef in Coconut Milk

Coconut milk gives a lovely creamy flavour to this spiced beef dish. ☺ ☺

    2 tablespoons oil
    1 cup beef spice paste (page 42)
    600 g (1¼ lb) beef topside, cut in
        2.5 cm (1 in) cubes
    2 stalks lemon grass, bruised
    2 *salam* leaves
    5 cm (2 in) *laos*, peeled and chopped
    1 litre (4 cups) water
    1 litre (4 cups) coconut milk
    fried shallots to garnish

Heat oil in heavy stock pot. Add spice paste and fry over low heat for 2 minutes. Add beef cubes, lemon grass, *salam* leaves, *laos* and water. Bring to the boil, reduce heat and simmer until meat is three-quarter cooked (approximately 40 minutes).

Add coconut milk, bring to the boil, reduce heat and simmer until meat is tender and sauce thickens. Season to taste with salt and pepper.

Garnish with fried shallots. Serve with steamed rice and a sambal.

Helpful hints: If you want to prepare this dish in advance, do so just up to the stage before you add the coconut milk. Be sure not to cover the pan once you have added the coconut milk or the sauce may curdle.

SEMUR LIDAH

Ox Tongue in Sweet Nutmeg Sauce

Although native to Indonesia, the nutmeg is not often used in cooking. One exception is the braised meat dish known as *Semur*, which is generally made with beef. This Balinese version uses ox tongue and partners the inimitable fragrance of nutmeg with sweet soya sauce. 🕐 🕐

2.5 litres (10 cups) water
600 g (1¼ lb) ox tongue, washed well
3 cups beef stock (page 41)
4 tablespoons sweet soya sauce
2 tablespoons thin soya sauce
¾ teaspoon ground white pepper
¼ teaspoon freshly grated nutmeg
3 fragrant lime leaves
3 tablespoons fried shallots
3 medium-sized potatoes, peeled and cut in 2 cm (¾ in) dice
fried shallots to garnish

Bring water to the boil in a heavy stock pot, add whole ox tongue and bring back to the boil. Reduce heat and simmer for approximately 1 hour or until tongue is nearly cooked. Strain stock and cool tongue down to room temperature. Peel skin off with a sharp knife.

Slice ox-tongue in thin even slices and place in saucepan. Fill up with beef stock and add both lots of soya sauce, pepper, nutmeg, lime leaves and fried shallots. Bring to the boil, reduce heat and simmer for 10 minutes. Add potatoes and continue to simmer until potatoes are cooked.

Garnish with fried shallots.

Helpful hints*:* The flavours of this dish seem to intensify if it is kept and reheated; add the garnish only when serving.

KAMBING MEKUAH

Balinese Lamb

Goat is more likely to be used than lamb in Bali to make this curry-like dish. 🕐🕐

> **600 g (1¹/₄ lb) boneless lamb leg or shoulder, cut in 2 cm (³/₄ in) cubes**
> **2 tablespoons oil**
> **1 cup basic spice paste (page 41)**
> **1 teaspoon coriander seeds, crushed**
> **1 tablespoon distilled white vinegar**
> **12 whole cardamom pods, bruised**
> **1 stalk lemon grass, bruised**
> **1¹/₂ cups water**
> **2 cups coconut milk**

Bring 3 litres (12 cups) of water to the boil in a large pot. Add lamb cubes, cook for 5 minutes then pour off the water.

Heat oil, add the spice paste and coriander and fry for 2 minutes over medium heat. Add lamb, cardamom, lemon grass and 1¹/₂ cups water. Bring to the boil and simmer until three-quarters cooked.

Add coconut milk, bring back to boil and simmer uncovered until meat is tender. Should the sauce reduce too much, add a little chicken stock. The sauce should be creamy in consistency.

Serve with steamed rice or compressed rice cakes, fried shallots, lemon slices and sliced celery.

Helpful hints: The lamb can be replaced by either beef or chicken.

SATE LILIT
Minced Seafood Satay

This is probably the most delicious satay you'll ever encounter. The delicate flavours of the prawn and fish are greatly improved if you can find spears of fresh lemon grass to use as skewers, and if you can cook them over a fire of coconut husks rather than charcoal. Nonetheless, even with wooden skewers and a standard charcoal grill, you'll have people coming back for more. ☺☺☺

300 g (10 oz) skinned boneless snapper fillet
300 g (10 oz) raw prawns, peeled
2 cups freshly grated coconut, or 1½ cups
   dessicated coconut, moistened
½ cup seafood spice paste (page 42)
5 fragrant lime leaves, cut in hair-like shreds
1 teaspoon black peppercorns, finely crushed
2 teaspoons salt
3–5 green bird's-eye chillies, very finely
   chopped
2 tablespoons brown sugar
lemon grass, cut in 15 cm (6 in) lengths, or
   satay skewers

Combine snapper fillet or other firm white fish with prawns and mince very finely in a food processor or with a chopper. Add all other ingredients and mix well.

Mould a heaped tablespoonful of this mixture around a wooden skewer or over trimmed stalks of lemon grass and grill over charcoal until golden brown.

Helpful hints*:* It is important to use fresh prawns and fish for this dish, as thawed frozen seafood exudes too much moisture. The brown sugar not only adds a touch of sweetness but helps give the slightly charred exterior typical of Balinese satay.

SATE SAMPI & SATE UDANG

Beef Satay & Prawn Satay

SATE SAMPI

Balinese satays are always a little charred on the outside, which gives them a particularly delicious flavour. Once the meat is marinated, it can be kept fresh for at least 4 days in a refrigerator. 🕐🕐

*Opposite:
Bottom left: Beef Satay; bottom right: Minced Seafood satay; top left: Prawn Satay; top right: Chicken Satay.*

600 g ($1^1/_4$ lb) beef topside,
   cut in 1 cm ($^1/_2$ in) cubes
3-5 bird's-eye chillies, chopped
2 tablespoons brown sugar
$^1/_2$ cup beef spice paste (page 42)
satay skewers

Combine meat, chillies, brown sugar and spice paste and mix well. Cover and marinate for 24 hours in refrigerator. Spear four pieces of meat very tightly on a satay skewer. Place satays on charcoal cooker and grill over very high heat either on coconut husks or on charcoal. Serve with satay sauce.

To make satay with lamb, pork or duck, follow the directions above but use basic spice paste (page 41). If using chicken, replace with chicken spice paste (page 42).

SATE UDANG

Lemon grass used as a skewer imparts a wonderful flavour to the inside of the prawns; if it is not available, substitute with normal satay skewers. 🕐🕐

600 g ($1^1/_4$ lb) large prawns, peeled
1 cup seafood spice paste (page 42)
fresh lemon grass, cleaned and cut
   15 cm (6 in) lengths

Combine prawns and seafood spice paste and mix well. Cover and marinate for 24 hours in refrigerator. Spear each prawn on the thinner end of a lemon grass stalk. Grill over very high heat, using either coconut husks or charcoal.

Helpful hints*:* Satays make a delicious cocktail snack, or can be the star of any barbecue. If using split bamboo or wooden skewers, soak in cold water for an hour before using to help prevent them getting burned.

SIAP MEPANGGANG & SIAP MEGORENG
Grilled Chicken & Fried Chicken

Grilled or fried chicken often forms part of the elaborate temple offerings and appears at most traditional ceremonies. Simmering it in spiced coconut milk before grilling or frying imparts a very special flavour.

SIAP MEPANGGANG

This is one of Bali's most traditional dishes and plays an important role in many ceremonies. ◔◔

    4 baby chickens, each 400 g (13 oz)
    1 cup chicken spice paste (page 42)
    2$\frac{1}{2}$ cups coconut milk
    3$\frac{1}{4}$ cups chicken stock (page 46)
    4 stalks lemon grass, bruised
    4 *salam* leaves
    1 tablespoon salt
    1 tablespoon black peppercorns, crushed

Cut along the backbone of chicken, open butterfly style and flatten. Heat a heavy saucepan, add spice paste and sauté for 2 minutes over low heat. Add coconut milk, chicken stock, lemon grass and bring to boil and simmer for 5 minutes. Add chickens and simmer until three-quarters cooked, turning chicken frequently.

Remove from fire and cool chicken in the sauce to room temperature. Remove chicken from sauce and dry well in open airy place for 30 minutes. Grill over charcoal until dark golden brown.

Grilled chicken tastes best when served with peanut sauce, steamed rice and vegetables.

SIAP MEGORENG

For Balinese fried chicken follow the same steps described above. Rather then grilling over charcoal, fry in medium hot oil until golden brown. ◔◔

Helpful hints: The chickens can be simmered in coconut milk and then deep-frozen until required. Be sure to dry them thoroughly after defrosting, either in an airy place or in front of a fan, before grilling or frying.

AYAM PELALAH

Shredded Chicken with Chillies and Lime

You can use any type of left-over chicken (roast, steamed or fried) for this delightfully tangy chicken salad. ⊘ ⊘

1 whole chicken, weighing about 1.2 kg
(2¹/₂ lb)
1 cup chicken spice paste (page 41)
¹/₂ cup Sambel Tomat (page 44)
3 tablespoons freshly squeezed lime juice

Rub the chicken outside and inside with the spice paste. Place on wire rack in oven and roast at 180°C (350°F) until done. When cool, remove and discard the skin. Remove meat from bones and shred by hand into fine strips. Combine chicken strips with remaining ingredients. Mix well and season to taste.

Serve at room temperature with steamed rice.

Helpful hints: Should there be any left-over chicken, it can be mixed with mashed potato and made into patties; just shallow fry them in a little hot oil until golden. The use of potato is not strictly Balinese, but the result is very good.

SIAP BASE KALAS

Chicken in Spiced Coconut Milk

Why simmer food in stock or water if you can use the rich, creamy milk squeezed from the flesh of grated coconuts? The Balinese use coconut milk for cooking everything from vegetables to seafood, meat to dessert bananas and, as in the following recipe, for lovely chicken curries. 🕐🕐

2 tablespoons oil
1 cup basic spice paste (page 41)
1 stalk lemon grass, bruised
1 *salam* leaf
1 kg (2 lb) chicken, cut in 8 pieces
1 teaspoon salt
$^{1}/_{2}$ teaspoon black peppercorns, crushed
1 litre (4 cups) coconut milk
fried shallots to garnish

Heat vegetable oil in heavy saucepan. Add spice paste and sauté for 2 minutes over low heat. Add lemon grass, *salam* leaf and chicken pieces and continue to sauté for 2 minutes. Season with salt and pepper.

Pour in coconut milk, bring to boil and simmer until chicken is cooked and sauce thickens. If sauce becomes too thick, add a little chicken stock. Serve with Nasi Kuning or steamed rice.

Helpful hints: Do not cover the pan during cooking to prevent the coconut milk from curdling. If you are worried about cholesterol, discard the chicken skin before cooking.

BEBEK BETUTU

Roast Duck in Banana Leaf

The rich flavour of duck is greatly enhanced by a host of pungent roots, herbs and seasonings in this dish, which is invariably a great favourite with visitors to Bali. The Balinese have great admiration for the duck and consider it to be a particularly strong animal as it is, like the turtle, the only one able to survive on land as well as water. 🕐🕐🕐

1 whole duck, about 2 kg (4$\frac{1}{2}$ lb)
18 shallots, peeled, cut in half and sliced
6 cloves garlic, peeled, halved and sliced
3 stalks lemon grass, finely sliced
5 fragrant lime leaves, finely sliced
6 candlenuts, chopped
5 cm (2 in) ginger, peeled and chopped
8 cm (3 in) fresh turmeric, peeled and chopped
8 cm (3 in) *kencur* root, peeled and chopped
1 teaspoon black peppercorns, crushed
5 bird's-eye chillies, sliced
1 teaspoon coriander seeds, crushed
2 teaspoons dried shrimp paste, roasted and coarsely crushed
1$\frac{1}{2}$ tablespoons salt
3 tablespoons oil
banana leaves, greaseproof paper or aluminium foil for wrapping

Wipe the duck dry and set aside. Combine all ingredients except banana leafs in a bowl and mix well. Rub the duck outside with this mixture and fill the centre of the duck with the remainder. Close open duck with satay skewer. Wrap in several layers of banana leaves, greaseproof paper or foil and steam for 50 minutes. Transfer duck to a moderate oven and bake at 180°C (350°F) for 30 minutes.

Remove banana leaves, cut duck meat up in small pieces and serve with stuffing. When cooked, the meat should be so tender that it falls off the bones.

Helpful hints: The flavour of this excellent duck will be even better if the final roasting is done over a slow charcoal fire rather than in the oven; be sure to turn the duck several times if cooking over charcoal.

TUM BEBEK

Minced Duck in Banana Leaf

Almost any type of meat, such as pork, duck, chicken, beef and even eels can be minced up and highly seasoned to make tum, one of the most popular dishes in Balinese homes. Try this version and you'll understand why. 🕐 🕐

600 g (1¼ lb) boneless duck, skin removed and minced
1 tablespoon fried shallots
1 tablespoon fried garlic
⅓ cup coconut milk
3 tablespoons basic spice paste (page 41)
4 bird's-eye chillies, sliced
1 tablespoon salt
1 teaspoon black peppercorns, crushed
12 pieces banana leaf, cut in 20 cm (8 in) squares

Combine the above ingredients except for banana leaf and mix well. Put a heaped tablespoon of the mixture into the centre of a banana leaf and wrap as described on page 29. Steam parcels for about 15–20 minutes, until well cooked.

The above mixture can also be used for duck satays; simply add 600 g (1¼ lb) of grated coconut and double the quantity of the basic spice paste, salt and pepper. Spear 2 heaped tablespoons of the paste on a large satay skewer or stalk of lemon grass.

Helpful hints: If banana leaves are not available, replace with aluminium foil.

SAMBEL BE TONGKOL
Tuna Salad

The emphatic flavour of tuna marries well with the tangy seasonings in this recipe. You can substitute fresh tuna with canned tuna chunks; season the tuna as directed but do not attempt to fry it. ☺ ☺

4 fresh tuna steaks, weighing 100 g (3$^1/_2$ oz) each
$^1/_4$ cup seafood spice paste (page 42)
1 teaspoon salt
$^1/_2$ teaspoon black peppercorns, crushed
1 tablespoon freshly squeezed lime juice
2 tablespoons oil
1 cup Sambel Matah (page 44)
fried shallots to garnish

Season fresh tuna steaks with seafood spice paste, salt, pepper and lime juice. Heat oil in frying pan and cook tuna steaks for 3 minutes on each side over high heat. Do not overcook. Set aside and allow to cool down, then break the tuna into small chunks. Place in salad bowl, add Sambel Matah and mix well.

Season to taste with salt and pepper and garnish with fried shallots. Serve at room temperature with steamed rice.

Helpful hints: Any other firm, well-flavoured fresh fish such as snapper, sea bass or salmon can be substituted for tuna.

BE PASIH MEPANGGANG

Marinated Grilled Fish

The fragrance of seasoned fresh fish sizzling over charcoal is almost irresistible. This recipe comes from the popular Ulam restaurant in Buala village, not far from the 5-star hotels of the southern resort area of Nusa Dua. ⏲

1 kg (2 lb) whole snapper, cleaned
2 tablepoons freshly squeezed lime juice
1 teaspoon salt
1 teaspoon powdered white pepper
1 cup seafood spice paste (page 42)
oil to brush fish

With a sharp knife cut four slits about 2 cm ($\frac{3}{4}$ in) deep on both sides of the fish. This allows the seasoning to penetrate better and the fish to cook more evenly. Season outside with lime juice salt and pepper. Fill the inside of the fish with seafood spice paste. If possible, leave the fish to marinate for several hours to improve the flavour.

Brush with a little oil, place on charcoal grill and cook over medium heat. Serve with *Sambel Tomat, Sambel Matah* and white rice.

Helpful hints*:* As fish tends to stick very easily, be sure to oil both the fish and the grill liberally before cooking. If you used a hinged wire grilling rack that holds the fish firmly, it makes the cooking much easier and ensures the fish doesn't break up. Snapper can be replaced by any other whole white-fleshed fish suitable for grilling, such as perch or sea bass.

TAMBUSAN BE PASIH

Diced Fish Roasted in Banana Leaf

The banana-leaf wrapping keeps these roasted bundles of fish delightfully moist and helps prevent the fish getting burned when you place it directly on the charcoal. If you are using foil as a substitute, it is better to place the fish on a grill above the charcoal during cooking. ⊘ ⊘

600 g (1^1/$_4$ lb) boned mackerel fillets, skin removed and cut in 2.5 cm (1 in) cubes
^{1}/$_2$ cup basic marinade
1 heaped tablespoon tamarind pulp, soaked in ^{1}/$_4$ cup warm water and juice extracted
1 teaspoon black peppercorns, crushed
1^1/$_2$ teaspoons salt
3 fragrant lime leaves, cut in hair-like shreds
3 tablespoons oil
2 *salam* leaves
2 squares of banana leaf, 30 x 30 cm (10 x 10 in)

In deep bowl combine mackerel cubes, spice paste, tamarind juice, crushed black pepper, salt, lime leaf and oil, and mix very well in order to coat fish evenly. Cover and marinate in cool place for 2 hours.

Place one *salam* leaf in centre of each piece of banana leaf.

Top with half of seafood mix and fold the same way as for *Tum Bebek* (page 86). Place parcels directly onto moderately hot charcoal and roast very slowly for one hour. Alternatively, bake on a rack in a moderate oven or under a grill for about 30 minutes.

Serve with *Sambel Matah* (page 44), Sambel Tomat, wedges of lime and steamed rice.

Helpful hints: The parcels of fish can be prepared up to 24 hours in advance and refrigerated. Fish can be replaced by chicken if liked.

PESAN BE PASIH

Grilled Fish in Banana Leaf

This is the Balinese equivalent of a popular Javanese dish, *Ikan Pepes*. If banana leaves are not available, replace with greased aluminium foil. Small whole fish are often used in Bali instead of fillets cut from a large fish; just adjust the size of the banana leaf wrapping. 🕐 🕐

500 g (1 lb) skinned boneless snapper fillet, cut in 4
1 teaspoon salt
1 cup seafood spice paste (page 42)
8 sprigs lemon basil
4 *salam* leaves
4 banana leaves, cut in 15 cm (6 in) squares

Season fish fillet with salt and cover evenly with seafood spice paste. Cover and leave to marinate in cool place for 6 hours. Place fish in centre of banana leaves, top each with 2 sprigs of lemon basil and 1 *salam* leaf. Fold banana leaves around fillets in shape of a small parcel and fasten with a toothpick, as shown at the top of page 29. Steam parcels for 15 minutes, then place on charcoal cooker or under a grill and cook for 5 minutes until banana leaves are evenly browned.

Helpful hints: You can steam the packets several hours in advance before barbecueing.

IKAN LELE

Cat fish

The whiskered cat fish, though not an attractive looking creature, tastes excellent when cooked in this fashion. ◑ ◐

4 cat fish (ikan lele), weighing 350 g (12 oz) each
1 teaspoon salt
1 teaspoon black peppercorns, crushed
2 tablespoons freshly squeezed lime juice
1 cup seafood spice paste (page 42)
2 cups coconut milk
2 *salam* leaves
1 stalk lemon grass, bruised

Season cat fish with salt, pepper and lime juice and marinate for 30 minutes. Deep fry fish over medium heat for 10 minutes until crispy.

While the fish is marinating, combine all remaining ingredients in saucepan and bring to boil over medium heat. Reduce heat and simmer for 30 minutes until coconut milk breaks apart and sauce becomes oily and clear rather than creamy.

Pour the sauce over the fried fish and serve.

Helpful hints: If cat fish is not available, replace with any fresh whole fish or follow the same method with any boneless fish fillet.

SAMBEL UDANG

Prawn Sambal

Prawns, sold only in the coastal markets of Bali, and in the capital, Denpasar, are a rare treat for most Balinese. 🕑🕑

**400 g (13 oz) large prawns, peeled and
  cleaned**
pinch of salt
$^1/_4$ teaspoon powdered white pepper
1 tablespoon freshly squeezed lime juice
**4 tablespoons seafood spice paste
  (page 42)**
4 tablespoons oil
$^1/_2$ cup coconut milk
pinch of sugar
fried shallots to garnish

Season prawns with salt, pepper and lemon juice. Add spice paste and mix well. Heat oil in heavy saucepan or wok. Add prawns and sauté for 2 minutes over low heat while stirring continuously. Pour in coconut milk and bring to boil, reduce heat and simmer for 2 minutes or until sauce thickens. Season to taste with a pinch of sugar.

Garnish with fried shallots and serve with Coconut Rice, *Sambel Tomat* and fresh lime.

Helpful hints: You can use shrimps instead of large prawns, although it takes longer to peel them. If you like a generous amount of sauce, you can double the amount of coconut milk.

KENUS MEBASE BALI
Balinese Squid

If you're only accustomed to eating deep-fried squid, you'll be surprised by the difference when its is cooked Balinese style. If squid is unavailable, replace with large cuttlefish or any other firm fish fillets such as snapper or sea bass. ☯☯

600 g (1¼ lb) baby squid
1 tablespoon freshly squeezed lime juice
⅓ teaspoon powdered white pepper
½ teaspoon salt
3 tablespoons oil
5 shallots, peeled and sliced
2 large red chillies, seeded and sliced
½ cup seafood spice paste (page 42)
1 cup chicken stock (page 46)
5 sprigs lemon basil, sliced
fried shallots and sprigs of
    lemon basil to garnish

Remove skin of squid and pull out the tentacles and head. Cut off and discard the head and beaky portion, but reserve the tentacles if preferred. Clean the squid thoroughly inside and out. Marinate squid with lime juice, pepper and salt.

Heat oil in wok, add shallots, chillies and squid and sauté for 2 minutes over high heat. Add seafood spice paste and continue to sauté for 1 more minute. Pour in chicken stock, add the sliced basil and bring to boil. Reduce heat and simmer for 1 minute. Season to taste and garnish with sprigs of lemon basil, fried shallots and serve with Coconut Rice (page 31).

Helpful hints: If you are using frozen squid, plunge in boiling water for 30 seconds to seal the squid, thus ensuring that it will sauté rather than stew.

NASI GORENG

Fried Rice

There are about as many different ways of preparing *Nasi Goreng* in Bali as there are cooks. The only constant ingredient is rice; everything else is determined by the cook's taste or the availability of ingredients. Noodles, introduced by the Chinese, have become a favourite in Bali as well as elsewhere in Indonesia. For *Mie Goreng* (Fried Noodles), substitute 750 g (1½ lb) fresh yellow noodles for the rice and follow exactly the same method. ⏱

6 tablespoons oil
6 shallots, peeled, halved lengthwise and
    sliced
6 cloves garlic, peeled and sliced
200 g (6½ oz) chicken meat, sliced
150 g (5 oz) medium-sized shrimp, peeled
¼ small white cabbage, shredded
4 eggs, beaten
½ cup *Sambel Tomat* (page 44)
750 g (1½ lb) cold cooked rice
2 teaspoons salt
1 tablespoon sliced bird's-eye chillies
2 tablespoons fried shallots

Heat vegetable oil in wok or heavy frying pan until very hot. Add shallots and garlic and fry for 1 minute until golden yellow. Add chicken and shrimp and fry for 1 minute, then add cabbage and fry for 1 minute. Add *Sambal Tomat* and mix well.

Add eggs and continuously stir for 30 seconds. Increase to very high heat, add rice and salt. Fry for 3 more minutes, stirring continuously. Add chillies, mix well and serve immediately, garnished with fried shallots.

Helpful hints: The cooked rice must be absolutely cold to make sure it does not become soggy during frying. It is important to have the heat under your wok at the absolute maximum when frying the rice.

NASI KUNING

Yellow Rice

Yellow, one of the four sacred colours, makes this festive rice dish strikingly different from the normal, everyday steamed rice. The rice is cooked in lightly seasoned coconut milk and chicken stock for extra flavour, while the touch of oil in the coconut milk gives it a glistening appearance and keeps each grain separate. ⏱

$1^{1}/_{2}$ cups long-grain rice, washed and drained
$2^{1}/_{2}$ cups coconut milk
$^{3}/_{4}$ cup chicken stock (page 46)
1 *salam* leaf
1 *pandan* leaf
1 stalk lemon grass, bruised
2 tablespoons turmeric water (page 37)
2 cm ($^{3}/_{4}$ in) *laos*, cut in 4 lengthwise slices
1 tablespoon salt

Combine all ingredients in rice cooker or heavy stockpot and simmer, covered, until done.

Helpful hints: If you are not using a rice cooker, cook the rice over high heat until the liquid comes to the boil, then lower heat and cook gently so that the coconut milk does not catch and burn on the bottom of the pan. Remove the lemon grass and *laos* before serving.

JUKUT NANGKA MEKUAH & SAYUR PAKIS

Young Jackfruit with Coconut Milk & Fern Tips in Garlic Dressing

JUKUT NANGKA MEKUAH

If jackfruit is not available, substitute with summer squash, winter melon or turnip. 🕐🕐

> **750 g (1¹⁄₂ lb) young jackfruit, peeled, cleaned and cut in pieces 2.5 x 1 cm (1 x ¹⁄₂ in)**
> **1 litre (4 cups) chicken stock**
> **¹⁄₂ cup vegetable spice paste (page 44)**
> **4 cups coconut milk**
> **2 teaspoons salt**
> **¹⁄₂ teaspoon black peppercorns, crushed**
> **fried shallots to garnish**

Bring 3 litres (12 cups) of lightly salted water to the boil. Add jackfruit, bring back to the boil, then reduce heat and simmer for 15 minutes. Drain water and rinse jackfruit in ice water.

Heat chicken stock, add vegetable spice paste and jackfruit and bring to the boil. Add coconut milk and simmer, stirring continuously, until jackfruit is tender and stock thickens a little.

Season to taste with salt and pepper and garnish with fried shallots.

SAYUR PAKIS

Fern tips—inexpensive and gathered wild—have a delightful, spinach-like flavour. 🕐

> **400 g (12¹⁄₂ oz) young fern tips or spinach**
> **3 cloves garlic**
> **4 cm (1¹⁄₂ in) *kencur* root, peeled and chopped**
> **4–7 bird's-eye chillies**
> **2 tablespoons oil**
> **¹⁄₂ teaspoon salt**
> **¹⁄₄ teaspoon black peppercorns, crushed**

Blanch fern tips in boiling water and cool under running water. Drain and dry thoroughly.

Place all remaining ingredients in a food processor and blend coarsely, or grind in a stone mortar. Combine this mixture with the vegetables and mix well. Serve at room temperature.

Helpful hints: The fern tips and the seasonings can be prepared in advance and combined just before serving.

LAWAR

Green Bean Salad with Chicken

No big religious or private celebration would be held without serving this ritual dish. Only the eldest, and most experienced men are allowed to mix the many ingredients. ⊘ ⊘ ⊘

3 cups blanched long beans cut in $^1/_2$ cm
($^1/_4$ in) slices
$^1/_2$ cup grated coconut, roasted
6 clove garlic, peeled, sliced and fried
6–8 shallots, peeled, sliced and fried
2 large red chillies, seeded and cut in fine strips
4–6 bird's-eye chillies, finely sliced
3 teaspoons fried chillies
(*Sambel Sere Tabia*, page 44)
2 tablespoons chicken spice paste (page 42)
fried shallots to garnish

Dressing:

250 g ($^1/_2$ lb) boneless chicken, minced
2 tablespoons chicken spice paste
1 teaspoon freshly squeezed lime juice
1 teaspoon salt
$^1/_2$ teaspoon black peppercorns, crushed
banana leaf, cut in 30 cm (12 in) square

Combine beans, coconut, garlic, shallots, all the chillies and chicken spice paste in a large bowl and mix well.

To prepare the dressing, combine chicken mince with 2 tablespoons of chicken spice paste and mix well. Place minced chicken lengthwise in centre of banana leaf and roll up very tightly. Place banana leaf roll on aluminium foil and roll up again very tightly. Turn sides simultaneously in opposite directions to tighten the roll. Steam roll for 20 minutes. Remove aluminium foil and banana leaf, break up meat with a fork to its original minced form.

Combine minced chicken with bean mixture, season to taste with salt pepper and lime juice. Garnish with crispy fried shallots.

Helpful hints: The minced chicken can be replaced by beef, pork or shredded young jackfruit.

TIMUN MESANTEN & BUAH KACANG MEKUAH
Cucumber with Coconut Sauce & Long Beans

TIMUN MESANTEN

The bland flavour of cucumbers can be enhanced when prepared with coconut milk and spicy seasonings. ⊘

- 2 tablespoons oil
- 3 shallots, peeled and sliced
- 2 cloves garlic, peeled and sliced
- 2 large red chillies, seeded and sliced
- $\frac{1}{2}$ teaspoon dried shrimp paste
- 2 cups coconut milk
- 1 teaspoon salt
- $\frac{1}{4}$ teaspoon black peppercorns, crushed
- 2 medium-sized cucumbers, peeled, seeded and sliced
- fried shallots to garnish

Heat oil in heavy saucepan. Add shallots, garlic and chillies and sauté for 2 minutes over low heat. Mix in shrimp paste and sauté for another minute. Pour in coconut milk and bring to the boil. Reduce heat and simmer for 5 minutes.

Add cucumbers and bring to a boil. Reduce heat and simmer until cucumbers are cooked and sauce thickens. Garnish with fried shallots.

BUAH KACANG MEKUAH

This soupy vegetable dish has plenty of savoury liquid which can be spooned over rice. ⊘ ⊘

- 2 cups chicken stock (page 46)
- $\frac{1}{2}$ cup basic spice paste (page 41)
- 1 stalk lemon grass, bruised
- 3 *salam* leaves
- 600 g ($1\frac{1}{4}$ lb) long beans, cut in 2.5 cm (1 in) pieces
- fried shallots to garnish

Heat chicken stock in saucepan. Add basic marinade, lemon grass and *salam* leaves and simmer for 5 minutes. Add beans and bring to the boil. Reduce heat and simmer until beans are cooked. Season to taste with salt and pepper. Garnish with fried shallots.

Helpful hints: Any type of green bean can be used instead of the long Asian variety.

JUKUT BLIMBING

Star Fruit Leaves in Sweet Sauce

Starfruit trees grow in many Balinese gardens, a convenient source of leaves for vegetable dishes. The leaves are crunchy with a slightly bitter tang. If not available, substitute with spinach leaves. ⏲ ⏲

    400 g (13 oz) starfruit leaves, washed
    ¹/₂ cup basic spice paste (page 41)
    2 cups coconut milk
    2 *salam* leaves
    300 g (10 oz) beef rump, minced
    ¹/₄ teaspoon black peppercorns, crushed
    ¹/₂ teaspoon salt

Bring 3 litres (12 cups) of lightly salted water to boil in stockpot. Add starfruit leaves, reduce heat and simmer for 5 minutes. Drain leaves then cool to room temperature in ice water. Drain and dry well. Place half of the marinade into saucepan and sauté for 2 minutes. Add coconut milk and *salam* leaf, reduce heat and simmer until sauce thickens.

Season minced beef with the remaining basic marinade. Place on to banana leaf and roll up very tightly into the shape of a sausage. Steam for 15 minutes. Allow to cool, open banana leaf and break meat into its original minced consistency.

Mix the coconut milk and minced beef well and add starfruit leaves and mix again. Season to taste with salt and pepper. Serve at room temperature with steamed rice.

Helpful hints*: You can steam the meat in a small covered dish if preferred.

JUKUT URAB

Mixed Vegetables with Grated Coconut

Although mixed vegetables are used in this version of Urab, it is possible to make it with 400 g (14 oz) of just one of the vegetables listed; spinach can also be used. ⏱⏱

- 100 g (3¹/₂ oz) blanched cabbage
- 100 g (3¹/₂ oz) spinach, blanched
- 100 g (3¹/₂ oz) long beans, cut in 2.5 cm (1in) pieces, blanched
- 100 g (3¹/₂ oz) bean sprouts, blanched
- 1 large red chilli, sliced
- 1 tablespoon grated coconut
- 2 tablespoon fried shallots

Dressing:

- 2 tablespoons fried shallots
- 2 tablespoons sliced garlic cloves
- 1 large red chilli, seeded and sliced
- 2 teaspoons fried chilli (Sambel Sere Tabia, page 44)
- 3 fragrant lime leaves, very finely sliced
- 4 cm (1¹/₂ in) *kencur,* peeled and chopped
- ¹/₄ teaspoon salt
- ¹/₄ teaspoon crushed black pepper
- ¹/₂ teaspoon white sugar
- 1 tablespoon oil

Cut cabbage into pieces about 2.5 cm by 1 cm (1 in by ¹/₂ in). Mix all vegetables, chilli, grated coconut and fried shallots in salad bowl and mix well.

For the dressing combine all ingredients and mix well in separate bowl. Mix the dressing thoroughly with the vegetables, season to taste with salt, pepper and lime juice. Serve at room temperature.

Helpful hints: If you are using fresh coconut, you will need to discard any left-overs as the coconut will turn sour within a few hours.

RUJAK

Vegetable and Fruit Salad with Palm Sugar Sauce

This popular snack, an intriguing mixture of sweet, sour and spicy hot flavours, is prepared at countless warung throughout Bali. 🕐🕐

1 small pineapple, peeled and sliced evenly
1 sour mango, peeled and sliced
1 pomelo or grapefruit, peeled and cut in segments
1 small cucumber, peeled, seeded and sliced
3 water apples (*jambu*), quartered (optional)
1 medium-sized starfruit, sliced
½ small papaya, peeled, cut in half, seeded and sliced in even segments
1 green apple, peeled and sliced
1 cup Rujak Sauce (page 46)

Combine all ingredients in salad bowl and mix well. Serve at room temperature.

Helpful hints*: Although this is served as a snack in Bali, you can serve it as part of a Balinese meal or buffet.

WAJIK & PANCONG

Rice Flour Cake with Palm Sugar & Coconut Cake

WAJIK

There are a couple of variations on this popular cake, which can be stored in the refrigerator for several days. It is normally served at room temperature, but can also be served warm topped with coconut milk. Another variation is to add ripe diced jackfruit (or substitute with sultanas) after the rice is partially cooked. 🕐

> 1 cup glutinous white rice
> 1 cup water
> 1 pandan leaf
> $\frac{1}{2}$ cup palm sugar syrup (page 36)
> $\frac{1}{4}$ cup thick coconut milk
> pinch of salt

Rinse rice very well under running water for 2 minutes and soak for 4 hours. Rinse again until water becomes clear. Place rice, 1 cup of water and pandan leaf in rice cooker or steamer and cook for approximately 20 minutes or until liquid has evaporated.

Add palm sugar syrup, coconut milk and salt, and steam for 15 minutes. Spread rice evenly 2.5 cm (1 in) thick on tray and allow to cool to room temperature. Wet a sharp knife with warm water and cut into even squares to serve.

Helpful hints: To speed up the soaking process, pour boiling water over the rice and let stand for 1 hour. Drain, then add another lot of boiling water and soak for another 30 minutes. If you are using a steamer to cook the rice, line the bottom with a wet cloth to prevent the rice grains from falling through.

PANCONG 🕐🕐

> 2 cups freshly grated coconut, or $1\frac{1}{2}$ cups dessicated coconut moistened with warm milk
> $\frac{1}{3}$ cup glutinous rice flour
> $\frac{1}{3}$ cup plain rice flour
> $\frac{1}{4}$ cup white sugar
> $\frac{1}{2}$ teaspoon salt

Combine all ingredients in a deep bowl and knead well for 3 minutes until the dough is smooth and does not stick.

Dust a cake tin with a little rice flour and press the dough into it. Bake in moderate oven (180°C / 350°F) for approximately 35 minutes or until the top is golden brown.

JAJA BATUN BEDIL

Sticky Rice Cake in Brown Sugar Sauce

The uninteresting appearance of this dessert belies its delightful flavour and creamy texture. ☻ ☻

Dumplings:

   1 cup glutinous rice flour
   ¹/₂ cup tapioca flour
   ³/₄ cup water
   ¹/₄ teaspoon salt

Make dumplings first. Place rice and tapioca flour in deep mixing bowl and make a well in the centre. Add water and salt, mix well and knead dough until it can be rolled and shaped. Dough should not be too dry. Roll small dumplings 1 cm (¹/₂ in) in diameter. Bring 4 litres (8 cups) of water to boil. Add dumplings, bring back to the boil and simmer for 5 minutes. Drain and set dumplings aside.

Sauce:

   3 cups water
   1 cup coconut milk
   ¹/₃ cup palm sugar syrup (page 36)
   1 *pandan* leaf
   pinch of salt

To make sauce, combine water, coconut milk, palm sugar, *pandan* leaf, and pinch of salt in small stockpot. Bring to boil. Add flour dumplings and simmer for 20 minutes.

   Cool and serve at room temperature.

Helpful hints: When preparing the dumplings, use the amount of water given in the recipe only as a guideline; the quality of flour varies greatly and affects the amount of liquid it absorbs. Add sufficient water to result in a soft, smooth dough. If the dumplings are dry when shaped, they will be very tough after cooking.

BUBUH INJIN

Black Rice Pudding

It's hard to find a foreign visitor to Bali who does not fall in love with the wonderful nutty flavour and meltingly smooth texture of Black Rice Pudding, served with a swirl of creamy coconut milk on top. ⏱

1 cup black glutinous rice
³/₄ cup white glutinous rice
2 *pandan* leaves
5 cups water
¹/₂ cup palm sugar syrup (page 36)
1¹/₂ cup freshly squeezed thick coconut milk

Rinse both lots of rice thoroughly for 2 minutes under running water. Drain. Put 5 cups water, both lots of rice and *pandan* leaf into heavy pan. Simmer over medium heat approximately 40 minutes.

Add palm sugar syrup and continue to cook until most of the liquid has evaporated. Season with a pinch of salt. Remove from heat, allow to cool. Serve at room temperature, topped with freshly squeezed coconut milk.

Helpful hints: As fresh coconut milk turns rancid fairly quickly, a pinch of salt is usually added to the milk to help preserve it for a few hours. A more effective alternative is to cook the coconut milk with 1 teaspoon of cornflour diluted in a little water; heat gently, stirring constantly, for a couple of minutes. This coconut sauce will keep overnight.

Milk made from instant powdered coconut will not turn rancid, although the flavour is not as good as fresh coconut milk.

GODOH & PISANG RAI
Fried Bananas & Boiled Bananas

GODOH

Fried bananas are popular throughout Southeast Asia, where they are abundant and inexpensive. The slow frying technique used in this recipe ensures that the bananas remain crisp after cooking. ⏱

1 cup rice flour
²/₃ cup water
¹/₄ teaspoon salt
8 small finger bananas
oil for frying

Place rice flour in deep mixing bowl. Make a well in the middle of the flour, and add water and salt. Whisk vigorously until batter is evenly smooth for coating and not too thin (if too thin, add more rice flour).

Peel bananas and cut in half lengthwise. Dip into batter to coat generously. Heat oil in wok or deep fryer until moderately hot. Add bananas and fry slowly until golden brown and crispy. This will take about 15 minutes. Remove bananas from oil, drain on paper napkins and dry well. Can be served with *Unti* (page 128).

PISANG RAI

Follow same steps as above for the batter. Coat bananas generously. Bring 1.5 litres (6 cups) very lightly salted water to the boil with a *pandan* leaf. Add bananas and boil over very low heat for approximately 10 minutes. Drain on clean kitchen towel. Coat evenly with freshly grated coconut. ⏱

Helpful hints: Add a pinch of salt to the grated coconut to help it remain fresh.

KOLEK PISANG

Finger Bananas in Coconut Milk

There are more than a dozen types of edible banana in Bali; this dessert uses the tiny sweet variety about 10–12 cm (4–5 in) in length. ☻

3 cups coconut milk
½ cup palm sugar syrup (page 36)
1 *pandan* leaf
16 finger bananas, peeled
1 tablespoon cornflour
1 tablespoon water

Bring coconut milk, palm sugar syrup and *pandan* leaf to the boil over medium heat. Reduce heat and simmer for 15 minutes. Add finger bananas and continue to simmer for 10 minutes.

Dissolve cornflour in water and add to bananas. Continue simmering for a couple of minutes, stirring until the sauce thickens. Remove from heat, discard *pandan* leaf and allow to cool. Serve well chilled.

Helpful hints: If you cannot obtain the tiny finger bananas, use regular sized bananas cut diagonally in 10–12 cm (4–5 in) lengths.

DADAR
Coconut Pancake

These pancakes, with a sweet coconut filling known as Unti, are a popular snack food and also sometimes eaten for breakfast. ☉

    100 g (3$\frac{1}{2}$ oz) rice flour
    2 tablespoons sugar
    $\frac{1}{4}$ teaspoon salt
    3 eggs
    1 cup fresh coconut milk
    2 tablespoons oil

Combine rice flour, sugar, salt, eggs, coconut milk and coconut oil in a deep mixing bowl. Stir well with whisk until all lumps dissolve. Strain through strainer. Batter should be a very liquid in consistency. Heat non-stick pan over low fire. Add 4 tablespoons of mixture and fry very thin pancakes. Cool pancakes down to room temperature.

Unti:

    1 cup fresh grated coconut
    $\frac{1}{2}$ cup palm sugar syrup (page 36)
    1 *pandan* leaf

To make the filling, combine sugar syrup and grated coconut and mix well. Add *pandan* leaf and fry over low heat in frying pan for 2 minutes stirring continuously. Cool and use at room temperature.

Place 1 tablespoon of coconut filling in centre of each pancake, fold at edge and roll tightly into tube shape.

Helpful hints*:* Both the pancakes and the filling can be made in advance and refrigerated; allow both to come to room temperature before filling.

Index

Alphabetical List of Recipes